STEVE NASH

DAVE FESCHUK AND MICHAEL GRANGE

STEVE NASH

THE UNLIKELY ASCENT OF A SUPERSTAR

RANDOM HOUSE CANADA

PUBLISHED BY RANDOM HOUSE CANADA

Page 203 is a continuation of this copyright page.

Library and Archives Canada Cataloguing in Publication

Feschuk, Dave
Steve Nash : the unlikely ascent of a superstar /
Dave Feschuk and Michael Grange.

Includes bibliographical references and index.
Issued also in electronic format.

ISBN 978-0-307-35947-6

1. Nash, Steve, 1974–. 2. Basketball players — Canada — Biography.
3. Success — Psychological aspects. I. Grange, Michael II. Title.

GV884.N37F48 2013   796.323092   C2013-900623-0

Cover and text design by Jennifer Lum

Cover image: © Noah Graham / National Basketball Association /
Getty Images

Printed and bound in the United States of America

2 4 6 8 9 7 5 3 1

To our families

CONTENTS

INTRODUCTION

It was a February night in Los Angeles and Steve Nash's Lakers were beating their ancient rivals from Boston. Up 81–65 with just under five minutes to go in the third quarter, Nash made an efficient if unthreatening feed from the right wing to Lakers forward Antawn Jamison, who promptly turned, shot and scored. And with that simple transaction, Nash passed Magic Johnson for fourth place on the NBA's all-time assists list.

There was no ceremony. There wasn't much to-do. But it was the kind of occasion that prompts sporting giants to take stock. After the game Lakers coach Mike D'Antoni was compelled to offer some insight into the stuff that made Nash one of the great players in basketball history.

"Just his mastery of the fundamentals," D'Antoni said. "He's a lot stronger and more athletic than people give him credit [for being]. Because you look at him and say, 'He's normal.' But he's not normal."

That his looks can deceive is one of the essential truths of Nash's incredible climb from ambitious Victoria high-schooler to surefire Hall of Famer. He looks normal because he's a man of relatively modest proportions playing a game populated by genetic aberrations, but his story most certainly is not. He's a Canadian who learned the fundamentals in a small Canadian city excelling in a sport perfected and still dominated by Americans groomed by the best collegiate basketball system in the world. At 18, a little more than two decades before he'd compiled a resume that includes two NBA MVP trophies, he was an unknown quantity in a landscape often given to prodigies, able to convince precisely one NCAA Division I head coach to offer him a spot on a team.

Nash has lasted seventeen seasons in the NBA's high-altitude power game, but he's a master of subtler arts performed well below the rim. Vision, feel, an uncanny instinct for team dynamics—these are some of his weapons. But he's also a crowd thriller in his own right. His is one of the great shooting strokes in the history of the NBA; and the area beyond the three-point line is one of his comfort zones. For a man who has defined himself as a brilliant passer—as a collegian, Johnson once called him "Little Magic"—his best theatre has come during those shining moments in which he has decided to become an unrepentant scorer.

In perhaps his greatest offensive performance—a 48-point explosion in the 2005 NBA playoffs as a member of the Phoenix Suns—Nash showcased every nuance of a skill set honed during countless hours of solitary communion between boy, ball and rim. He was playing against the Dallas Mavericks, the franchise that had balked at signing him to a long-term contract a summer earlier for fear his then 30-year-old body couldn't weather the rigours of another long season, let alone another multi-year contract. A few months past his 31st birthday, he looked awfully healthy. He swished his lean-back fall-away jump-shot. He made his left-handed floater, his spot-up three-pointer and his dime-stop crossover foul-line pull-up. He hit his fake-left, fake-right step-through lay-in. He made a shot as he careened at high speed toward the cameramen on the baseline, his body out of bounds before the high-arcing work of art found the bottom of the net. The Mavericks tried bigger defenders, stronger ones, quicker ones. But again and again Nash (who has spent a career showing that straight-line speed isn't necessarily as dangerous as changing speeds) used slow-fast hesitation drives to open up the space he needed to operate.

Watching the broadcast now, you can still hear the play-by-play man's astonishment: "How easy can it get?!"

In truth, it's rarely been easy for Nash, even if, in his best moments, he makes a complicated puzzle look simple. He struggled in his early days at Santa Clara University. He was a third-stringer in his first year as a pro. He was booed by the home crowd in his first season as a starter in Dallas. But struggles can be overcome, Nash has shown the world, if you go to work every day and vow to get a bit better.

Nash came into the NBA as a good shooter, but he'll leave it as one of the finest to ever loft a ball at a rim. No player has been more accurate from the free-throw line (he and Mark Price are the only players to shoot better than 90 percent from the charity stripe for their respective careers). When Nash missed two consecutive free throws during a game in the 2012–13 season, Hubie Brown, the great former coach and broadcast analyst, proclaimed his shock: "I nearly fell off the couch." Indeed, Lakers centre Dwight Howard missed more free throws in the 2012–13 season than Nash has missed in his entire career. Nash is one of only a handful of men in the 50–40–90 Club—that is, players who shot 50 percent from the field, 40 percent from three-point range, and 90 percent from the free-throw line in the same season. Larry Bird did it twice. Nash has done it four times. Nobody else has done it more than once. And if you broaden the criteria just a bit, Nash's excellence is even more telling—an NBA player has shot 39–49–89 (not as catchy, but still remarkable accuracy from all three spots) just 24 times while playing at least 24 minutes a game, and Nash is responsible for seven of them.

Nash's list of accomplishments in the years since he made a series of clutch free throws to help Santa Clara pull off a memorable upset of Arizona in the NCAA tournament is gaudy and unfathomable. Eight times he's played in the NBA All-Star Game. Only one other Canadian has played in the game, Toronto's Jamaal Magloire, and he made it once, as an injury replacement. Seven times he's been a member of the All-NBA Team, including three seasons on the starting five. Two times he's been named regular season MVP. Nash will be counted among the greatest Canadian athletes in history. Many of his peers in those ranks have defined themselves on a hockey rink, but there have been few Canadians who've proven themselves superior in a sport with a truly global talent pool, let alone one in which the great power to the south takes nationwide interest, and he's done it at point guard, the one position in basketball where sheer size doesn't automatically narrow down the pool of applicants; it's the most competitive position in the sport.

Nash is also an Olympian, an entrepreneur, a filmmaker, a philanthropist and an executive—general manager of Canada's senior men's national team, a role that has him curating the team he once led on a thrilling run to the medal round at the 2000 Sydney Olympics.

No, he's definitely not normal. But neither is he magic. He fought through an injury-riddled season with the Lakers in 2012–13, and when the results of a late-season MRI revealed the not-so-inspiring state of the chronic back trouble that has dogged the majority of his pro career, he had to succumb to a painkilling epidural injection in the hopes of performing in the playoffs.

As for playing hurt, maybe he'll be remembered best, when the evidence of his thousand-plus games gathers dust in the archive, for a single act of perseverance. It happened in the final few minutes of Game 1 of the 2007 Western Conference semi-finals, after Nash's nose was split open in a head-to-head collision that floored Spurs point guard Tony Parker. It was an ugly scene. The blood refused to stop flowing and as it seeped from beneath Nash's bandages, the Spurs couldn't stop him. Though his eyes stung from the blood-clotting chemical liberally applied by a trainer, he stayed in the game and made a series of crucial plays. He let fly with a three-pointer that tied the game with a couple of minutes to go. He drained a lunging scoop shot. No less than Don Cherry, hockey's voice of manliness, would laud him for his gore-stained brilliance.

What Nash did that day was the same thing he's done from the beginning: keeping at it even when it looked like he had no place in the game.

CHAPTER ONE

Victoria: You Never Know When You're in the Right Place

The gymnasium of Sudbury's Lockerby Composite School is a long way from having Jack Nicholson cheer you on from the sidelines at the Staples Center. A teenage basketball player in the mid-1970s couldn't start much farther from the glitz and narcissism of the Hollywood crowd the Los Angeles Lakers are charged with entertaining than shooting hoops in a Northern Ontario mining town best known for the Big Nickel. But so unlikely is the journey Lakers point guard Steve Nash has taken to earn $9 million a year directing traffic for the most glamorous basketball club in the world, it may as well start there, in a butterfly-flapping-its-wings kind of way, with a couple of kids who never would make the NBA.

The scene: A kid named Dave Zanatta is shooting hoops. He's visiting from Sault Ste. Marie, another northern town four hours away, playing some pick-up basketball with friends. Eli Pasquale, Sudbury's best, is in the gym too. It's summer and it's hot. Someone suggests going to the lake to swim. Eli says, "Sure, why not," and off he goes. Zanatta says "no thanks" and keeps shooting in the heat.

A few hours later Pasquale comes back and finds Zanatta still at it; still banging off jumpers and working on his weak hand. Pasquale feels a flush in his cheeks—a combination of anger, regret and shame. A decision is made.

"That was it, I said 'never again,'" he recalls nearly thirty-five years later. "I made a decision at that point—I think in Grade Eleven—that never again was I going to let anyone else play more hours than I do. And I don't think many did, to be honest. Kids laugh, but they don't realize it. I put in six to eight hours a day. That's what I did in the summertime. There was no question. I put my time in."

Pasquale had bigger things in mind, distant, magical goals.

The butterfly flaps its wings again, pushing our tale a little closer to Los Angeles: In 1975 the Canadian men's basketball team played an exhibition game at Maple Leaf Gardens in Toronto against Russia and it was carried live on CBC, the first time ever a basketball game featuring the Canadian men's team had been broadcast nationally. It was a big moment in the same way that anything Canada-Russia was big in the wake of the 1972 Summit Series in hockey. Canada won 86–84, the first time Canada had ever beaten the USSR in hoops. At home in Sudbury, Pasquale, then a five-foot-something point guard no one had ever heard of in a town the basketball cognoscenti would never be able to find, watched it and made another decision. "I saw it on TV. It was broadcast on CBC or CTV or whatever—one of the two channels—and for whatever reason it just hit me: I want to go to the Olympics, I want to play for Canada. So that was my start of that."

———

"Where are you from?"

It's a big question. There is the physical aspect: where you were born and took your first steps. For Steve Nash that was Johannesburg, South Africa, and Regina, Saskatchewan. But then there's the bigger part of the question—what place shaped you as a person? Where did enough things fall into place that they set you on a path to your destiny, or at least, in retrospect, your destination? For Nash that place is Victoria, B.C. But if you want to understand why a jewel of a city on Vancouver Island was the right place for him to begin his NBA moon shot, it's worth knowing a few things. Among them is that Eli Pasquale—aspiring Olympian, once and never again bested by Dave Zanatta—left his hometown of Sudbury in 1979 to pursue his own basketball destiny in Victoria and helped shape the place Nash calls home. Pasquale and Ken Shields, the coach he followed there, had an impact on Victoria, and that was both by making basketball matter in the B.C. capital, and proving that big dreams pursued in a faraway place can come true. And Victoria, a city then on exactly no college basketball program's radar? Victoria shaped Nash.

The athleticism of Steve Nash is one of the least-discussed elements of his long list of sporting attributes. Only in the NBA, where athleticism is defined on a superhuman scale, does Nash get lumped in as "average" or worse. It's almost certain that another sport or two could have led to professional riches had he chosen a path other than hoops. His brother, Martin, played soccer professionally, and Nash was just as good growing up. Could he have followed his neighbours growing up—Geoff and Russ Courtnall—into a long NHL career? It doesn't seem that far-fetched. How about rowing? Could he have been an Olympian oarsman, like so many who passed through his hometown? Maybe he'd have the appetite for that particular suffer-fest of a sport; maybe not. But it's not hard to make the case that rowing helped propel Nash to NBA stardom.

Allow us to explain—again the butterfly's wings move with the most unpredictable results. Unlike Nash, Silken Laumann, a Canadian Olympic hero and world champion rower, had all the physical tools to be an elite basketball player. She was not only tall at 6-foot-1, she was incredibly strong, her broad-shouldered athletic frame easily carrying 165 pounds of hard-packed muscle at her sporting peak. She was an excellent distance runner, rare for a woman of her size, who was competitive in high school cross-country and even during her rowing career was renowned for tacking on a nineteen-kilometre run at the end of a week's training on the water and in the weight room. Whether those extra kilometres were the ones that pushed her over the top and helped her earn Canada a World Championship and three Olympic medals, you can only speculate. But the focus and determination required to leg out that extra distance were entirely evident as she delivered one of Canada's most memorable sporting moments of the past twenty-five years.

Laumann was in the final stages of her preparation for the 1992 Olympics when her leg was gored in a freak collision with another rowing shell. The knife-like point of the boat shredded her leg down to the bone. Her Olympic career was almost certainly over; her ability to run or even walk normally again suddenly in doubt. She was hospitalized for three weeks and underwent five surgeries. But determined to race, Laumann had her rowing shell specially outfitted to accommodate her injured leg, got back on water and against all odds earned a bronze medal in Barcelona barely ten weeks after her accident. The feat was one of the most powerful stories to emerge out of the 1992 games and catapulted Laumann—already one of Canada's most recognizable Olympic athletes—into the stratosphere of fame usually reserved for star hockey players.

But for all of that, she's well aware of her limitations. And among them is that she can't play basketball; not a lick. She did play on a team once, for Lorne Park Secondary School in Mississauga, Ontario, but it was not a positive experience. In her first game, she grabbed a rebound and eagerly put it back up, feeling a visceral thrill when it dropped through the hoop. But the feeling was fleeting, snuffed out by the realization she'd scored on her own basket.

"That was pretty much the end of my basketball career," says Laumann, laughing.

But it wasn't the end of her effect on basketball. Not even close. Basketball's loss was rowing's gain and the University of Victoria's fortune; with the trickle-down making it to a certain Steve Nash, budding basketball superstar, whether or not he ever touched an oar.

It was a scene worth at least a smile. First of all there was the costume: a puffy collection of robes and a floppy velvet hat that fell somewhere between what a shady character in a 1970s blaxploitation flick might wear and a court jester's outfit. Nash couldn't help himself when he walked across the stage of the Farquhar Auditorium to accept an Honorary Doctor of Laws degree at UVic's 2009 graduation ceremony. That he was wearing sneakers only added to the look. He was touched, certainly, but his irreverent sense of humour remained intact. "What a privilege," he said. "And not just for the outfit."

He was in some ways a surprising choice for an honorary degree, given he'd been by his own admission a less than enthusiastic high school student and had enrolled at the University of Santa Clara with a priority on mastering basketball, though he did squeeze in a sociology degree along the way.

But the University of Victoria shaped his hometown in many ways and for a kid growing up just a short bike ride from campus, it had helped shape an athletic world view that ultimately proved global in scope.

When Nash started to follow basketball, he studied Magic Johnson and Isiah Thomas on television, but coverage wasn't as ubiquitous then as it is now; there were no YouTube highlight packages. Fortunately he had a real-life role model close at hand in one Eli Pasquale. The kid who made up his mind to be great one burning hot summer day in Sudbury had found his way across Canada.

Nash hadn't yet got serious about basketball when Pasquale was wrapping up one of the finest careers in Canadian university sports. The hard-working Italian kid from Northern Ontario had followed coach Ken Shields from Sudbury's Laurentian University to Victoria and was a five-year starter for the UVic Vikings, who were—not coincidentally—for those same five years, national champions, part of a run of seven straight titles. Pasquale was the Canadian player of the year when he graduated in 1984, and had established himself as the definitive Canadian national team point guard—until Nash came along a decade later.

While Pasquale was playing on the national team, it was the UVic campus where teenaged Nash went to basketball camps and snuck in after hours to work on his game. It was also where Shields, the Canadian national team coach, gave that high school kid a chance to practice with the best players in the country, Pasquale among them.

"I spent not a lot of time studying at [UVic] but enough hours in that gymnasium to play a few careers for the Vikes," Nash said as he was getting his honorary degree. "Growing up in Victoria it was hard to get time in a gymnasium. It was such a rare treat to have free time in a gym; we would break the law to get the opportunity and it's well-documented how my friends and I would sneak into McKinnon Gym or jimmy the locks in the old gym across the parking lot so we could come back after dark on Friday night and let loose.

"I have a sense of pride and thankfulness for Victoria and in particular the university."

The Steve Nash Story as told on network broadcasts and in magazine profiles has always included some reference to the unlikeliness of his path to multiple most valuable player trophies and a place in the pantheon of NBA point guards. Close your eyes and you can hear it: "and all of this from a skinny white kid from Victoria, British Columbia, on Canada's far west coast, a place known for oceans and mountains, but not for producing NBA players."

When he was named an NBA All-Star for the first time in 2003, rare was the story that didn't mention his shortness, whiteness, Canadianness and lack of jumpingness, often in the first couple of paragraphs. He was the guy who didn't fit in; the guy not from the hard streets of some U.S. city or a place dripping with basketball tradition like North Carolina or Indiana or Kentucky. He wasn't even the product of a European professional club's leading-edge academy system. He was from a place known for its climate, its status as a retirement destination and for afternoon tea at the Empress Hotel.

"It wasn't ideal, but what is ideal?" Nash said of his basketball home. "I continually found ways to inspire and motivate myself. I always looked up to the great players on TV, tried to follow their footsteps, do the same thing they did."

The idea of Nash overcoming his background—that he became a basketball star in spite of where he was from—is a cliché that defies logic. The reality is there is nowhere that can claim to be an assembly line for Hall of Fame talent. A glance at the list of players that Nash shares the MVP award with reveals a handful of multiple winners but no towns that have produced more than one MVP. Larry Bird is the only MVP from French Lick, Indiana. Michael Jordan is the only MVP from Wilmington, North Carolina, Dirk Nowitzki is the only one from Würzburg, Germany, and LeBron James is the only one from Akron, Ohio. The presumption that growing up in Victoria was an obstacle sells short the town and obscures lessons that can be learned about what manner of environment nurtures top talent.

And while Victoria might not jump off the map as an obvious exporter of NBA stars, it really was an ideal place for Nash to become one of the best to have ever dribbled a basketball. To be an impressionable, athletic kid growing up on the lush city's fields, parks, yards and school grounds was to see and feel greatness at every turn.

Being your best in Victoria wasn't about being the best in British Columbia or even in Canada. In Victoria it was fairly routine to mingle with athletes who numbered among the best in the world. Playing basketball at UVic wasn't a default option for kids who couldn't get a Division I scholarship. It was an honour bestowed on those who aspired to play internationally and professionally. National championships were a given while learning the game under the gaze of Ken Shields, one of the most respected coaches in the sport when it came to the game's technical aspects. Further, he expected that his best players would compete at an Olympic level; doing so wasn't treated as some abstract goal but a reality carved out through effort and precise applications of will.

When those from outside Victoria get immersed in the city's anything-is-possible culture for the first time, most are shocked when the apparent backwater refuses to take a backseat to any person or place.

"My wife has been wondering what's in the water here for the twenty-six years she's known me," says Jeff Mallett, president and chief executive officer of a start-up called Yahoo! Inc. during the early days of the Internet boom. One of Canada's most successful business exports, Mallet grew up in the same neighbourhood as Nash and attended the same middle school and high school, albeit ten years earlier than his eventual friend and business partner.

He may not have had the same athletic gifts as Nash, but Mallett had enough to play on a national championship soccer team at UVic and the provincial team, and to receive a scholarship at San Francisco State University. He also had the drive to become a millionaire many, many times over in the rough-and-tumble Darwinian-style capitalism of 1990s Silicon Valley. Does he love Victoria? Presumably. His oldest daughter is named after his hometown.

"My take-away is that it's something to do with it being an island and you have to make an effort to go elsewhere and so everyone understood you were going to bump into people and I remember coaches, teacher, parents—everyone seemed to be helpful and supportive, it was very communal. And if someone broke through, in sport or business, it was a community where people loved that."

Steve Nash's Victoria was a community that seemed to inspire great achievement. At its heart was the university and at the heart of the university was its athletic facility. It wasn't much to look at: the McKinnon Building is a massive, grey concrete slab of the type favoured by architects commissioned to design hospitals, prisons and schools in the mid-1970s. But its lifeless exterior belied the hum of human kinetic energy that crackled inside. When not honing her rowing technique on the water of Elk Lake, Silken Laumann spent a lot of her time at McKinnon for one important reason: it was a place she could go and fit right in as an 18-year-old aspiring Olympian and a UVic frosh whose idea of a good time was the Kiss the Whale Run—a weekly tradition where rowers, a few cross-country runners and even some basketball players (by nature loath to do any running when a ball is not involved) would meet on Friday afternoons and run from the campus to the town aquarium. At the entrance they'd kiss the statue of an orca whale, turn around and head back—a sixteen-kilometre loop. It was only when they'd finished that the kegs would start flowing in the "train hard, party hard" tradition of rowing.

"We tend to make success at anything about mystique or make it a science," says Laumann, who'd followed her older sister, Daniele, to the school from their native Mississauga, Ontario, and became the youngest member of Canada's burgeoning women's rowing program. "We analyze it to look for patterns. But in my experience it's pretty simple: It has a lot to do with hard work and being around people who believe in the possibility of success, and people who have been close enough to winning Olympic medals or on the world stage that they can help break it down. They make it real and map out a path of possibility."

Laumann's theory, based on intuition and personal experience, has been borne out by those who have devoted considerable effort to demystifying that skittering ball of mercury that we label, broadly, as talent. Determining where talent comes from and what it takes for talent to be realized has fascinated inquiring minds for millennia. It was Aristotle who piped up with "we are what we repeatedly do; excellence, then, is not an act, but a habit" and the speculation has been ongoing ever since. That's the line Daniel Coyle chose to start his book *The Little Book of Talent,* a companion to his larger study *The Talent Code,* in which he tries to drill down into the neurological and sociological aspects of talent development. His primary theme is that our brains are shaped physiologically as a result of what we undertake physically. As we practice certain activities—music, athletics, arts; nearly anything really—our brains are literally rewired. Efficiencies are created, our capacities increase and we improve. The well-worn "ten thousand-hour rule" cited by researcher K. Anders Ericsson as the root of world-class achievement (nearly without exception the best in any field have as a base ten thousand hours of intense practice to draw on) and popularized by Malcolm Gladwell is really just the moral of a story about brain development.

In visiting recognized hotbeds of success—the Spartak Tennis Club in Moscow, for example, which spawned Russia's female tennis revolution, or the tiny island nation of Curaçao, which has seen a disproportionate number of teams excel at the Little League World Series and a disproportionate number of players reach the major leagues—Coyle studies the factors that make each place *the* place in its chosen field. Some are more obvious than others. In the early days of the NHL, more hockey players came from Northern Ontario's mining towns than anywhere else, it seemed. It's not hard to figure out why: first of all it was colder for more months of the year, which meant more ice. And unlike many other remote places, the company towns had the resources and population to devote time and effort to teaching hockey to the town's kids.

A few generations later, kids from the north are increasingly rare in the NHL. Urban centres have long had the indoor rinks and financial demographics the game now requires. Once-fabled centres like Kirkland Lake are home to barely enough kids for a house league; most of the miners leave their families down south and rotate in and out of town on shifts.

Does Victoria measure up as a hotbed of world-class basketball talent? Not if the measure is how many kids from the B.C. capital made it to the NBA. Nash may forever be the only one. But the Victoria that he lived in had all kinds of opportunities for talent to flourish; perhaps the true nature of Nash's particular genius is that he was smart and determined enough to take advantage of the environment he was in, rather than lament what was missing. And one thing Victoria had was a commitment to excellence; basketball was just one avenue to achieving it.

Ten years after it opened in 1975, the McKinnon Gym was the nexus of one of the most significant concentrations of sporting talent Canada has ever seen, a depth and breadth of commitment and ability that even the elite Division I sports factories in the National Collegiate Athletic Association would look upon with envy.

By the time classes started for the fall semester in 1984, no fewer than 40 athletes and coaches—this from a mid-size school with an enrollment of 5,500—had a pretty chewy story to share for their "what I did last summer" report, having spent most of August in Los Angeles competing for Canada in the Summer Olympic Games. By comparison UCLA, with an enrollment of 35,000, could count 56. The University of Michigan, the perennial Big Ten powerhouse with 46,000 students, sent 9 athletes to Los Angeles.

"There wasn't a Canadian national high performance centre for rowing," says Laumann. "There was the UVic rowing team. That's why I came to UVic. It wasn't so much this program and structure creating the excellence, it was the athletes themselves and the coaching. This was a place you went because you wanted to be part of something special. I was motivated by everyone's work ethic. I was already a super-hard worker and I know I inspired other people with my twelve-mile runs."

Laumann lights up when talking about her days at UVic, brightened by the memory of being surrounded with like-minded people, rowers and other athletes.

"It all centred around that little McKinnon Gym," she says. "There was this carpeted area in the middle where we would all stretch, and after classes, I would say after about three p.m., people would start gathering there to meet others to run or to go to the weight room. There was just constant activity."

To the young Laumann, it was nothing remarkable, just part of the environment she lived and trained in. "When you're already an Olympic athlete, you don't think about it from the perspective of everyone being so amazing," she says. "These are your friends and who you hang out with and party with on the weekend.

"It's more afterwards I realized I was in the middle of a culture of excellence."

UVic loomed large in B.C.'s capital city. Nash never attended UVic (his brother, Martin, briefly did and his sister, Joann, was captain of the women's soccer team), but in a city of just 75,000, the school was a part of everyone's life. The person who introduced Nash to the stage when he received his honorary degree was Carole Miller, mother of Chris Miller, his best friend, and Jenny Miller, who today runs his foundation. He grew up tearing around her house and twenty years later she's presenting him as a sporting legend in the making.

After the provincial government and the healthcare industry, UVic was the city's largest employer, and along with the provincial civil service created a strongly family-oriented culture. The workday ended by five, if not earlier, and combined with the fact that there was every stripe of minor sport to play in Canada's mildest climate, Victoria's kids enjoyed some special opportunities for sport.

But more than simply the climate or the culture was the orientation of the place.

"There are a whole bunch of pieces that go into the mosaic," says Ian Hyde-Lay, who coached Nash in Grades 11 and 12 at St. Michael's University School and played basketball alongside Pasquale at UVic. "There are about 300,000 people in the region but also it's not a big enough city to support any of the core pro franchises, so there's always been a huge emphasis on amateur sport at a very high level.

"When I played for the Vikes it was a hot ticket. For Steve back then there would have been a lot of opportunity. He would have been encouraged to play year-round in all sorts of sports. He did his baseball, he did his soccer, he did his lacrosse. He had a dab at rugby. The climate allowed all of those outdoor sports to function all year round.

"By the time he was ready to enter university, Division I was emerging as an option and the NBA had re-established its brand with Magic and Bird and Isiah Thomas and Jordan. But when he was young, UVic was it if you were a basketball player. Making that team in the mid-eighties was a pretty significant accomplishment."

Nash might have been the only NBA player to emerge from Victoria, but the number of world-class athletes with ties to the city is remarkable. Canada's most accomplished rugby player, Gareth Rees, was a UVic star in the 1980s and '90s. The Gait brothers—two of the best ever to play lacrosse—were Victoria products. Two of the starters on Canada's 1984 World Cup soccer team were from Victoria. And more recently, Ryder Hesjedal became the only Canadian to win one of cycling's Grand Tours with his victory at the Giro d'Italia in 2012.

"It's a prosperous town, affluent town," says Hyde-Lay, who has spent his entire adult life competing or coaching in Victoria. "It's not that there's not a lower middle class, obviously there is, but for a high percentage of kids there is money to support them; there is a culture of parents supporting their kids with money and time."

When the Nash family originally moved from South Africa, they settled in Regina, Saskatchewan. Had the family stayed there it's quite likely that hockey—which Nash excelled in but dropped when soccer and basketball became bigger parts of his already full sports plate—would have claimed him, so omnipresent is the sport on the Canadian prairies. But Nash's father, John, moved from Regina to Victoria when Steve was four. Their house in the Gordon Head neighbourhood was adjacent to the schoolyard where he would spend hours alone with a ball, working his way through elaborate shooting and dribbling routines. And the Nash family just happened to arrive in Victoria when Shields, head basketball coach and

athletic director at UVic, was constructing an athletic program the quality of which had never before been seen in
Canada—and hasn't been since.

"For any athlete, internal drive and skill set are of para-
mount importance but for any young athlete coming
through, it's good fortune if you happen to cross paths
with a committed, organized, dynamic coach. Ken Shields
was a huge influence and mentor in my life in that respect,
and for Steve," says Hyde-Lay.

Shields made the UVic basketball program international
in its ambitions and standards. The UVic Vikes won the
national university basketball championships seven straight
years between 1980 and 1986. Their roster was loaded with
major talents who never ventured south—as difficult as it
was for Nash to earn a Division I scholarship in the early
1990s, it was even harder a decade earlier. In the Los Angeles
Olympics, Canada finished just out of the medals in fourth
place with a team that featured four UVic players—nearly
half the roster. As the general manager of Canada's men's
national team Nash will have almost exclusively NBA or
European professional players on his roster; four CIS
(Canadian Interuniversity Sport) players from a single program on the national team will never happen again.

"The culture was one of excellence," says Shields, who
still lives in Victoria and was a consultant to Great Britain's
women's program at the 2012 Summer Olympics. (It
should be noted that Shields' wife, Kathy, who coached the
UVic women's program, enjoyed nearly identical success
to her husband, winning five national championships in
the same seven-year period.) "We weren't hiding behind
academics. The vice-president of the university was really

upset that we were so driven. He thought we were going to become an athlete factory and that grades would suffer and he commissioned a study to examine the grades of athletes because he thought we were pushing too hard. He found the grades for the athletes were higher than the mean for the university."

In Canada, where universities are publicly funded and full athletic scholarships don't exist, sports as a worthy expression of excellence and achievement was a radical notion. "We made no bones about it," said Shields. "There is no conflict here, but you have to make sacrifices. You can't have a great personal life and social life and be an athlete and be a student and be successful.

"The university decided that they would pursue the highest standard of performance in a small number of sports where we had a natural advantage and a ready supply of athletes in sports that were indigenous to the area. For example, Elk Lake was the only ice-free lake in Canada [and thus conducive to year-round training for rowers] and so UVic recruited Al Morrow, a bright young coach," says Shields. "The university made a commitment to high performance and I don't know of one other university that has made that commitment in Canada. It was a stimulating place to be in those years."

While Shields was well versed in the nuances of every type of basketball, he wasn't opposed to stealing ideas from other sports. And so the basketball lifer studied rowing, where a young Silken Laumann and her teammates were creating a world-class training base.

"We were so proud of the culture that we established at UVic, but the rowers' training regime was legendary, the volume they were able to do because they were in a non-weight-bearing sport, same with swimmers," Shields recalls. "But I remember saying, 'Why is it the rowers get the lake completely free?' Because they're going at six a.m., at daybreak. No one is there.

"So we started running two-a-days. And it spread. Every single team trained in the morning and trained after school."

The rowers may have set the tone, but it was the basketball players who created the buzz: rowers, after all, don't really have home games.

As the Vikings racked up championships and played in front of sold-out crowds at McKinnon Gym, an aura built up around them. Curiously, it didn't create a gap between the team and the other athletes or the greater community, it created a bridge.

"That whole environment around the basketball program and the whole athletic program Ken and Kathy and everyone else was putting together then, that infected me," says Mallett, who still gets goosebumps talking about playing soccer for UVic as a freshman and helping the Vikings win another national title. "As a little freshman soccer player it showed me that sports was big time, you could win, you could play on a national level, there was such a buzz and it affected everyone. You chop me up and that would be something that was embedded in my brain."

"One thing about UVic was it was a very special place for recognizing success. Ken Shields led a very special athletic department and is a very special man: very passionate and committed to the athletes," says Laumann. "It was all about giving the athletes the best opportunity and experience possible. He expected hard work and rewarded hard work."

One of Laumann's fondest memories was being recognized as UVic's athlete of the year in 1986 at the school's athletic banquet, an occasion organized by Shields to celebrate UVic's athletic excellence. "You could have knocked me over with a feather that he would even notice me. Yeah, I was working hard and coming early and staying late and all of those things, but Shields was a busy guy and he noticed me and recognized me, and the Victoria *Times Colonist* was there, reporting on us."

The city itself embraced the success of UVic's athletic program in a way that wouldn't have happened in Toronto or Montreal or Vancouver. "It was mind boggling to me," Laumann continues. "It's the right size to rally around someone doing something special and maybe in a city that's much larger that's harder to do."

As Nash was improving into a high school standout, the aura of excellence at UVic touched him directly in countless ways. The opportunities that opened up as a result were far beyond what would have been available to him anywhere else in Canada and arguably anywhere in North America. Having taken the reins of the men's national team in addition to his duties at UVic, Ken Shields held training camps in Victoria, on one occasion at Mount Douglas High School, where Nash played in Grade 10, before transferring the next year to St. Michael's University School.

After that move, Nash wasn't just the best teenaged player in town—he was a point guard with NBA dreams sharing a practice floor with the best players in Canadian basketball and their coach as they prepared to face the

U.S. Dream Team in the Tournament of the Americas Olympic qualifying event later that summer.

But how did Nash get on Shields' radar? Well, part of it comes back to the scale of the place. When Nash transferred to St. Michael's University School midway through Grade 11, it made the front of the Victoria *Times Colonist* sports section. In Nash's senior season, the *Times Colonist* high school sports reporter, Jeff Rud, personally covered thirty of the boarding school team's fifty-four games on their way to a provincial championship. Nash had been covered in such detail at home that Rud could still write a fact-filled biography of the local boy made good years later when Nash made the jump from Santa Clara University to the NBA.

But there was also a more intimate connection between the coach and the teenager. One of Ken Shields' favourite players was a tough point guard named Ian Hyde-Lay. He wasn't the best player to suit up for the Vikes during those dominant years, but he might have been the most committed. Hyde-Lay was the type of athlete who thrived under the intense training culture that Shields borrowed from the internationally successful rowers on campus.

Hyde-Lay's drive and determination earned him the role of captain of UVic's championship team in his graduating year. He subsequently went into teaching and was St. Michael's University School's head of physical education and senior boys' basketball coach when he learned Nash was transferring to the school.

Nash had to sit out his Grade 11 basketball season, according to transfer regulations, but the time wasn't wasted. Hyde-Lay was from the Ken Shields coaching tree and routinely opened the gym so the pair could work on enhancing Nash's fundamental skills. He also put in a good word for Nash with his old UVic teammate, Eli Pasquale, recently retired from the national team and running basketball camps in Victoria. Pasquale took Nash on as a counsellor, and in this way the butterfly edged Nash a little closer to his destiny.

In the years since that summer day in Sudbury when he had made up his mind to be the best he could be, Pasquale had fulfilled his promise. He'd never stopped working, never stopped pushing himself. According to Shields, the only conditioning drill Pasquale didn't win in his time with the Vikings came in his freshman year, when he finished second to Hyde-Lay in a 3.5-kilometre run. It was a display of deference, the rookie not wanting to show up the captain on the first day. He won every other test the rest of his five years.

Pasquale had developed into a superb player, good enough to be drafted in the fifth round by the Seattle SuperSonics in 1984. He nearly made the team, coached by NBA legend Lenny Wilkens, but Seattle ended up trading for Boston Celtics guard Gerald Henderson as Wilkens was uncomfortable going into the season without a veteran NBA point guard. Pasquale went to camp the following season with the Chicago Bulls, auditioning as the set-up man for Michael Jordan, a job that eventually went to John Paxson, a far superior shooter.

"I understood that Michael Jordan didn't need a point guard," says Pasquale. "They needed a guy who could spot up and shoot."

That was it for Pasquale's NBA dreams, but at the time

he didn't think too much of it. After leaving UVic he had given himself two years to make it to the NBA; otherwise his focus was the national team and playing professionally overseas. The NBA had never seemed realistic to him and hadn't even emerged as a possibility until the 1983 World University Games in Edmonton, when Canada won a surprising gold medal, upsetting a U.S. team in the final that included the likes of future NBA Hall of Famers Charles Barkley and Karl Malone.

Pasquale's performance that summer earned him some attention and led to him being drafted, but the tournament was the first time he really thought the NBA was an attainable objective. The men's national team, however, was a goal he'd had in mind since he was 15 and watched them play on the CBC. That was the goal that led him to follow Ken Shields to Victoria in 1977. And that was the goal that resulted in fifteen seasons as Canada's point guard, helping the Maple Leaf to a fourth-place finish in the 1984 Olympic Games and sixth in 1988, to go along with his five Canadian university championships.

Pasquale returned to Victoria, comfortable in the place where he had competed and trained. Over time he struck up a friendship with a young kid with big dreams that his old coach Ken Shields was so high on. The teenaged Steve Nash reminded him of himself, although even then the kid possessed an offensive arsenal that Pasquale recognized as superior to his own. They'd play one-on-one at McKinnon Gym, with Pasquale finally finding someone who wanted to be on the floor as long as he did. Those sessions made an impression on Nash. Even after reaching the pinnacle of the sport, Nash recognized Pasquale as a mentor and someone who could have reached greater heights had he been drafted into a better situation.

"He was a really good player; very smart, very efficient, competitive," Nash says of Pasquale one morning in the dim hallway of US Airways Arena in Phoenix, a lifetime away from Victoria. "Really solid. I'm sure you could throw him in an NBA game and [he would] not miss a beat."

But more than his example, Pasquale said to Nash just the right thing at just the right time.

"The great piece of advice he gave me was when I was working at his basketball camp in Victoria, and he drove me home and he said, 'If you want to play in the NBA, you should decide right now.'"

Pasquale was drawing on his own experience. He made up his mind to be an Olympian and it happened. He didn't really think about playing in the NBA and he never did.

"He had some great questions all the time," Pasquale said. "We'd be doing my camp and he'd always be asking about stuff and that's the one thing I told Steve. He worked as one of my coaches, it was his last year of high school or going into his last year. And I said the fact that I wanted to go to the Olympics and be on the national team became a goal for me in Grade 10. And I said, 'If you have any thoughts about wanting to make the NBA you have to decide at this moment. You have to decide now and figure out what you have to do and go for it.'

"There's no guarantee it's going to happen, but by not making those goals, you can almost guarantee it's not going to happen."

It most certainly happened for Nash. When he won his first MVP award, the city of Victoria wanted to erect a statue in his honour. Nash declined. Instead his foundation partnered with local charities to refurbish a basketball court. It was a thank you to the place that not only hatched his basketball dreams but allowed him to believe it was possible to be the best in the world.

Was Nash born in a hotbed of elite basketball with a clearly worn path to the NBA trod by previous stars who played for the right high school and the right summer league team; one of several to attend a big-name university as a much-heralded recruit en route to becoming a pre-ordained first-round pick?

Not even close.

But was he born in a community unique in Canada for celebrating the potential of local athletes to achieve great things on a world stage? Yes. Did he have junior high school and then high school coaches who were directly influenced by the man many consider the best technical coach that Canada has ever produced? Yes. Did that coach, Ken Shields, take a direct interest in Nash as a young player at a critical point in his development? Yes. Was he able to tap into the knowledge and experience—good and bad—of Eli Pasquale, the best point guard Canada had developed until Nash came along? Yes, again.

It's hard to trace a tempest back to the butterfly wing that started it, but it's still worth asking: was Victoria an obstacle to Nash becoming an NBA star, or the reason he made it?

"I think everyone comes from a unique background," Nash said of his hometown at his first NBA All-Star Game in 2002. "I know mine is not maybe typical of an NBA player. I think at the same time [an NBA career is] achievable.

"That's a good lesson, that things are attainable."

CHAPTER TWO

A Little Magic at Santa Claus State

The goal was stated, the groundwork was laid, and a path was charted. Steve Nash declared his intention to arrive in the NBA. But even if Victoria was a starting point that had its advantages, it's not as though Nash could simply type his longed-for destination into Google Maps and follow the directions. Becoming an NBA regular, as a Canadian, was still a bit like going to the moon as the citizen of a country with a fledgling space program.

Only a short list of Canadians had appeared in the league by the time Nash began his quest, and very few of those men bore biographical resemblance to the young point guard. Mike Smrek, from Port Robinson, Ontario, won two championship rings with the "Showtime" Lakers as Kareem Abdul-Jabbar's practice partner, while Jim Zoet, from Uxbridge, Ontario, played in seven games for the Detroit Pistons from 1982 to 1983, scoring 2 points. Both were seven-footers, an advantage Nash did not have. As the old scout's saying goes: "You can't teach seven feet." And it follows, too, that you can certainly get to the NBA a whole lot easier than the majority of the population if you're blessed with such a dimensional upside.

Another group of Canada's NBA pioneers had geographical edges on Nash—specifically, they'd been born in Canada but spent key developmental years in the U.S.

Bill Wennington, a seven-footer hailing from Montreal who played on three championship teams with the Michael Jordan–era Chicago Bulls, played his high school hoops in the U.S. So did Canadian citizens Stewart Granger, Ron Crevier and Ernie Vandeweghe. Vandeweghe was a Montrealer by birth who, at 6-foot-3, went on to a prosperous NBA career before he fathered an NBA All-Star named Kiki, who is not Canadian.

Canada also produced a small sample of NBAers during the pro game's early days. The first NBA game took place in Toronto, a 1946 tilt between the hometown Huskies and the New York Knickerbockers. (Fans of the since-departed Vancouver Grizzlies and ever-lamentable Toronto Raptors will point out that Canada hasn't hosted a significant NBA game since.) The likes of Gino Sovran, Hank Biasatti, Bob Houbregs and Norm Baker made up the NBA's Canadian contingent in the 1940s and 50s. But again, they hardly offered Nash a template to emulate, since they partook in the pro game when it was largely a part-time pursuit.

So what of the Nash archetype, the raised-in-Canada kid prized more for his skill than his length, who only shipped off to the U.S. when an opportunity to play in the NCAA's top division presented itself? That list of precedents was awfully brief. Lars Erik Hansen was born in Copenhagen, grew up in Coquitlam, B.C., and played briefly for the Seattle SuperSonics. Leo Rautins was a bred-in-Canada collegiate star at Syracuse University who, in 1983, was picked in the first round of the NBA draft. And if not for a string of knee operations—fourteen in total—he might have played his best pro years in the world's best league. Instead, Rautins' short NBA run was followed by a fruitful career as a European-based pro. Once again, each man stood out in part because they stood tall: Hanson was 6-foot-10 and Rautins was 6-foot-8, the latter's size combined with his skill making him perhaps the most buzzworthy Canadian basketball prospect until Nash came along.

That was the extent of the national heritage of NBA stays. Nash, in aiming to carve out a long NBA career as an average-sized point guard was travelling without a comparable compatriot to guide him.

No matter where you're born and raised, of course, the odds of making the NBA are always staggering. Millions of kids play high school basketball in North America. Thousands play in the NCAA. But at any given time only a few hundred are deemed worthy to take up a spot on an NBA roster. Of those, a mere few dozen turn their NBA experience into a multiple-contract career. There are more astronauts and brain surgeons and arena-touring rock stars roaming the planet than there are ten-year NBA veterans.

Simply earning a scholarship to a U.S. Division I program is to run enough of a gauntlet. Those who rise through the high school ranks to earn themselves a place among the bigger men on any given college campus are understandably chuffed and occasionally delusional. There's a belief that college is a stepping stone to the NBA: that, because these athletes caught the eye of the talent scouts who round up the world's best high school players and funnel them into the NCAA's three-hundred-some Division I teams, they're sure to pique the interest of the bird dogs who do the same for the thirty NBA clubs. But with every step toward that goal, huge swaths of players are culled.

Nash's dream to make the NBA wasn't delusional. But it was far-fetched. Which is why, when he arrived on the campus of Santa Clara University in the late summer of 1992, his presence was met with a certain amount of skepticism.

That Nash had landed at Santa Clara at all was something of a miracle. The most highly touted U.S.-based players of Nash's graduating high school class received stacks of letters and no end of phone calls from adoring coaches and recruiters, and the history of NCAA rules violations (at least the ones that have been brought to light by the occasional slip-up) suggests some of them may have received the occasional stack of cash in a brown envelope.

Though he would one day rise to be recognized as the world's greatest floor general, Nash didn't receive stacks of under-the-table money or fawning letters from coaches on the make. There's an old sporting phrase: "If you're good enough, they'll find you." Today, this is undoubtedly true for Canadian basketball hopefuls. In the age of YouTube and Twitter, secret prodigies don't exist. But two decades ago, there were more than a few blind spots in the scouting network. The U.S. basketball establishment only found Nash because his high school coach spent significant time and money sending letters to college coaches, urging them to consider the merits of a star player from the wilds of Canada's left coast.

How good was he as a Victoria high-schooler? It was, in some ways, difficult to say. Yes, his statistics were impressive. He averaged 21 points and 11 assists and 9 rebounds a game—nearly a triple-double. As a senior, he led his St. Michael's University School team to a provincial championship. He was named British Columbia's player of the year—in both basketball and soccer. But all of that meant next to nothing to the arbiters of excellence south of the border. A basketball player dominating a Canadian high school league had only slightly more credibility than a hockey player ruling the rink in Abu Dhabi.

SMU games weren't Nash's only means of exposing his talents to a wider world, though. As a high-schooler, he had played with a provincial all-star team in a summer tournament in Las Vegas. In a key game, the story goes, he missed a layup at the buzzer that could have won his team the game and set up a meeting with a team led by California-bred point guard Jason Kidd, who at the time was drawing attention from most of the major U.S. college programs and whose eventual decision to attend the University of California was national news. If Nash had made that shot, his entire career may have played out in another way. Perhaps he would have gone from one of the game's best-kept secrets to one of its most-hyped, not-so-hidden gems. It didn't happen that way. Nash would one day be a teammate of Kidd's on the Phoenix Suns, not to mention the NBA's Western Conference All-Stars. But as high-schoolers, a blown layup kept them from meeting in competition.

And so it was left to Nash and his coach, Ian Hyde-Lay, to drum up American interest in Victoria's best high school player. Hyde-Lay wasn't well connected in NCAA circles.

But he had seen Nash practice with Canada's senior men's national team in the summer between Nash's Grade 11 and Grade 12 seasons and to his eye Nash had often looked like the best guard on the floor, bar none.

So, Hyde-Lay and Nash huddled. They drafted a list of thirty or forty U.S. colleges, looked at rosters, and surmised which ones might need a freshman point guard.

"Then I wrote to all the schools and said, 'I really believe there's a very special player here. A diamond in the rough. You really should follow through on this guy. Don't take my word for it. I know you have no idea who I am. But contact Ken Shields, the national coach. He'll give you a point of reference,'" Hyde-Lay has said. "And most—almost all of them—just blew it off."

The list of the uninterested is now the stuff of legend. Indiana wasn't interested, nor were Florida State, Duke, Villanova, Arizona, Washington, Pepperdine.

Tom Asbury, the Pepperdine coach when Nash and Hyde-Lay were on their fishing expedition, would later explain why Nash probably slipped through the screening apparatus: "When you're at Pepperdine, you get, oh, three hundred letters a year. And for a [six-foot-three] white guard from Canada, you're probably not going to do a lot of follow-up."

Virginia claimed they were intrigued enough to come and watch him play, but nobody from the school ever did. At least that was better than the lack of attention paid by the folks at the University of Washington; though they were just a ferry ride away, the Huskies never so much as wrote back.

"He's got a shoebox full of letters that say, 'Thanks but

no thanks,'" Hyde-Lay has said. "The most disappointing thing for me was thinking, 'Wow. This guy is really
good. And nobody even knows.' And I think Steve felt
the same thing."

As Nash would later tell *Sports Illustrated,* "The lack of
response hurt me, because I thought I was good enough
that people would come knocking on my door. It was like
I was trapped in an elevator and I'm screaming, but nobody
could hear me."

He wasn't, as it turned out, completely unnoticed. While
Nash's high school games went unwatched by college
scouts, he earned what turned out to be a key smidgeon of
exposure when, as a member of Canada's under-19 team,
he played in a friendly game against Long Beach State
University. Nash's play impressed a Long Beach assistant
coach, who mentioned the young point guard to his friend
Scott Gradin, who at the time was a volunteer assistant
coach at Santa Clara University. Gradin called Hyde-Lay
to request a videotape and received in return a jittery bit of
footage shot on a hand-held camera against questionable
opposition—"The Grainy Cult Video," as Hyde-Lay now
describes it. Nash so outstrips his competition therein that
at some points his fakes and dekes induce his defenders to
lose their footing in dramatic pratfalls. It was reminiscent
of watching the Harlem Globetrotters dominate the
Washington Generals.

"When I walked by the room where Scott was watching
the tape, he was laughing out loud," Dick Davey, then a
Santa Clara assistant coach, would say. "I asked him,
'What's wrong?' And he said, 'I got this tape of the Canadian
kid. He makes people fall down.'"

If the viewing of the tape induced get-a-load-of-this chuckles, it also inspired Gradin to request some better footage. And it soon inspired Davey to become the first and only U.S. Division I coach to venture to Victoria to watch Nash play in person. Davey, who said he was convinced after watching just the warm-up that Nash was worthy of a scholarship, called his wife before the game even started to express his hope that he was the only American recruiter in the gym.

"I was worried I'd see a coach from one of the bigger schools in the stands," Davey says. "And then I knew we wouldn't have a shot at him. But it turned out I was the only one there."

Nash achieved one of his key goals that night when Davey offered him a full scholarship. It came with a dose of criticism, though. The coach told Nash he was "the worst defensive player" he had ever seen. Davey would soon take over as Santa Clara's head coach, and that initial criticism would be a harbinger of a relationship that would include plenty of frank assessments of Nash's weak points. But, make no mistake, Santa Clara's coaching staff knew they'd stumbled across a major treasure.

"I really couldn't believe he was unrecruited," Gradin says. "When you watched him play, his ability to handle the ball, to break people down, to shoot it. It was impressive. And the thing that was most unique was his character. He was so selfless. Even in high school, he could have been far and away The Guy, The Star. But he shared the spotlight with some of his teammates. He'd tell you about his teammates. He'd very willingly defer. And I think that selflessness and humility was a unique characteristic, especially for an eighteen-year-old going into college."

The unrecruited unknown—it's a great story, and an uncommon one. Scottie Pippen, the Robin to Michael Jordan's Batman, wasn't a particularly well-known high school player. Part of the reason for Pippen's early anonymity was that when he shipped off to college, he stood all of 6-foot-2 and weighed 145 pounds—smaller than Nash at the same juncture. Pippen had sprouted to his full 6-foot-8 by the time he began to draw the attention of the few NBA scouts who were paying attention to the University of Central Arkansas. He would go on to be selected fifth in the 1987 NBA draft by the Seattle SuperSonics before being traded to Chicago, play seventeen NBA seasons, and become one of the headliners of the Dream Team—the U.S.'s fabled gold-medal-winning entry at the 1992 Barcelona Olympics. There'd be six championships in there, too—the credit for which largely goes to Jordan.

Pippen's brand of anything-is-possible narrative involved coaxing his pituitary gland into a 6-inch growth spurt in his late teens and suddenly packaging his point-guard skills in an NBA small forward's frame. But what of the players who haven't had the benefit of such freakish late-stage enhancement? There have been first-round-pick point guards who have flown under the high school radar. Andre Miller was an eighth overall pick in the 1999 NBA draft. And while he hardly grew up in a basketball backwater— he went to high school in his hometown, Los Angeles—he has long claimed that the University of Utah was his only real suitor. That's partly because Miller had the look of a pedestrian athlete. He also had trouble making the requisite score on his SAT, the NCAA's academic entrance test.

There are other out-of-nowhere tales. And the game certainly loves its zero-to-hero storylines. The fable marketers loved to perpetuate about Jordan was that he was cut from his high school team. The real story was a little more nuanced; the year he was "cut" was also the year he was assigned to the junior varsity squad—a customary move for a player of his grade level and relative stature. Jordan was, shortly thereafter, on the radar of a slew of post-secondary institutions, most notably the University of North Carolina, where as a freshman, Jordan hit the winning shot in the NCAA championship game.

The truth is it's always easy to pooh-pooh an unknown quantity, to look at a 6-foot-3 guard from Canada and say: "Not a chance." But Nash wasn't one to believe in such self-limiting sentiments and didn't pay much attention to the St. Michael's University School teammate who teased that he was headed to "Santa Claus State."

If Santa Clara didn't have much of a profile beyond the U.S. West Coast, it certainly had a long tradition. The small Jesuit school located on the southern tip of San Francisco Bay, a few kilometres from San Jose's airport, had an enrollment of about four thousand when Nash arrived. Only one alumnus had gone on to make a notable mark in the NBA: Kurt Rambis, the long-haired wearer of horn-rimmed spectacles who added hard-fouling grit to the high-flying Lakers of the 1980s.

One of Nash's early nemeses was junior John Woolery, the incumbent Santa Clara point guard. On the face of it, Woolery wasn't exactly a picture of intimidation. He was only 6-foot-1. He wasn't a great shooter. But Woolery was a specialist in his own right. He was possessed of

above-average quickness, relatively long arms and superior anticipation, and the combination put him among the
top ten in Division I for steals.

"I was a really good defender," Woolery says. "That
was what I could do. Being long and athletic, he just hadn't
gone against people like that. It was new to him."

It was also frustrating. There were many moments in
Nash's early practices at Santa Clara when the freshman
looked positively overmatched. At times Nash couldn't
dribble the ball over half court without Woolery forcing
him into a turnover. Woolery would steal the ball or force
Nash to dribble it off a foot or sail an ill-advised pass out
of bounds. The pattern got old quickly, and the mismatch
was stark enough that a Santa Clara coach had a conversation with Woolery.

"[He] called me in and said, 'Hey, ease up on him,'"
Woolery remembers. "But in my opinion, he was a fresh-
man guard and I was a junior guard. There was no way
I was going to ease up."

Nash, for his part, never asked for mercy or to be re-
assigned to a different check. Here was a teenaged kid in
a new city, setting out on a quest for world domination
and falling again and again at the first hurdle. He wasn't
bombing in his first game; he was bombing in his first
handful of practices. He wasn't being manhandled by a
seasoned pro; he was, as he would say later, having trouble
getting the ball over half court against somebody he'd
never heard of.

Woolery, who was defending his place on the team as
much as he was defending the basket, wasn't particularly
apologetic about causing his teammate so much grief. In

his earliest meetings with Nash, the Canadian had spoken matter-of-factly of his destiny as an NBA regular.

"It was kind of a laughable confidence at the time—not an arrogance, but he was just really sure of himself, of what he thought," Woolery says. "He felt for sure he was going to go to the NBA. At that time, you couldn't see it."

Woolery had played in high school against NCAA star Chris Mills, when Mills was California's state player of the year. A strong and athletic 6-foot-7, Mills was the kind of player for whose allegiance U.S. colleges would part with that proverbial envelope full of cash. (Mills actually found himself at the centre of a major recruiting scandal when a package addressed to his father containing $1,000 was linked to University of Kentucky assistant coach Dwane Casey, later the head coach of the Toronto Raptors.) Woolery had also played against Sean Higgins, a 6-foot-9 forward who would go on to help the University of Michigan to the 1989 NCAA championship.

"It's different with those guys, because you can see [the possibility of them making the NBA]. Their physical dominance—it was so obvious," Woolery says. "I think at the time of Nash's recruiting trip, he was five-foot-eleven, skinny. We played a little bit of pickup. He's not real athletic. He wasn't six-foot-seven, scoring forty points a game against other Division I players. So it was different."

Despite his skepticism and early dominance over the would-be NBAer, Woolery soon saw a side of Nash that was unique.

As Nash's frustration would grow, Woolery remembers him cursing in rage, slamming the ball to the floor and booting it toward the rafters to rue another turnover. But he doesn't remember Nash being deterred. Woolery would make a steal. Nash, like a kid trying to master a video game, would hit some kind of mental reset button and begin the battle afresh.

"Some guys in that same environment, even older guys, they would shy away from the ball. But he'd want to do it again and again and again. He'd wear me down in a way because he'd want to go at it again and again and again. He didn't care if it was the fifth time, the sixth time—he just wanted to do it over and over again, until he could get it right," Woolery says. "There were games when I could break a guy in the first half. I'd have eight or nine steals, and they would give in. That was an advantage. But there was no way he was going to give in. He'd be mad. He would fight and compete. The coaches would want to sub him out, 'No, I'm good. Let's go again.'"

Nash wasn't interested in running away from his failures; he was passionate about learning from them.

"He would ask me about things, 'What are you doing here? How should I do this? What do you see that I'm doing wrong?'" Woolery says.

The dominating junior wasn't the only one on whom Nash's refuse-to-lose competitive streak made an impression.

"You get a chessboard out and start playing chess—he's going to try and beat your ass," says Davey. "And it doesn't make any difference what it is—he has competitive drive at as high a level as I've seen. Almost every guy I've been around who has gone to the NBA has been that way. His is extreme, I think."

As it does with many hyper-combative types, Nash's competitive drive occasionally caused him to lose his patience in spectacular fashion—the sporting equivalent of overturning the chessboard.

"He definitely struggled with it," says Gradin. "He was a little homesick, I think. He started to question a lot of things. There were some obstacles. And I think at some point there was some doubt about whether he'd made the right decision to be there and be that far from home and everything that was familiar to him . . . When I think of Steve, I think of this upbeat, positive person. And although he wasn't a down guy, there was a period of time when he was in a funk."

There is no shortage of would-be NBA guards who, faced with a Woolery-esque roadblock, would have been exploring their transfer options. Nash didn't transfer. He transferred credit. He called Woolery "the heart of the team." And he laboured so that he might one day be in a position to be the same.

"He did a lot of after-practice stuff, either staying in the gym or coming back late at night. A lot of ball-skill things. Starts, stops, change of direction, left, right, spins, crossovers," Davey says. "He was good at that stuff anyway, but he got a lot better at it."

Nash wouldn't become Santa Clara's full-time starting point guard until his junior year—this after Woolery departed and Nash, in a ceremonial passing of the workaholic torch, made a point of acquiring the key to the gym that Woolery had previously been given by a caretaker. In the interim, Nash still managed to carve out playing time as a college rookie—not as a point guard, but as one of Santa Clara's most effective shooting guards.

The ability to shoot a basketball with accuracy from

distance is one of the great rewards the game bestows on its most dedicated practitioners. All those hours at the schoolyard and in the gym spent lofting a ball at a rim meant that Nash arrived on campus with at least one undeniable skill. Perhaps he lacked the physical strength and maturity to match up with the NCAA's best athletes. Certainly he lacked the game experience to be the on-court quarterback of a successful collegiate operation. But the object of the game is to put the ball through the hoop, and players with the ability to do that with efficiency, well, they're difficult to keep on the bench. So for all of Nash's faults, he still managed to play about twenty-four minutes a game in his first year at Santa Clara.

"Because he could shoot it so well, he had instant success as a freshman," Woolery says. "It kept him on the floor in tight games for some big-time experience."

That year the Broncos, under first-year head coach Dick Davey, put together an unimpressive 4–6 win-loss record in their non-conference schedule and were 3–4 through the first half of their fourteen-game regular season in the West Coast Conference, but gathered momentum as the season wore on. After they won six of their final seven league games, they came into the conference tournament as the No. 3 seed.

Thanks largely to some on-target three-point bombing, they defeated the likes of Saint Mary's, Gonzaga and Pepperdine to win the WCC tournament, and with it a berth in March Madness—the sixty-four-team NCAA tournament that Nash had watched on TV growing up. Nash was named the WCC tournament MVP, in part for making 15 of the final 19 three-pointers he took on the way to the championship.

Kareem Abdul-Jabbar, speaking as an analyst on ESPN, marvelled at Nash's poise: "For an eighteen-year-old freshman to be doing that well under this kind of pressure . . . I think we're seeing something very unique." Fans in the stands carried signs that read: "We are Nash-ty!" Years later the slang gurus at urbandictionary.com would remove the hyphen and provide the definition. "Nashty: When someone does something spectacular, amazing and/or unbelievable, like Steve Nash would do on the basketball court."

Said Nash at the time: "I don't know how to explain it. We just got on a roll. It was one of those extra-special weekends."

What the Broncos would do next remains an integral piece of collegiate hoops lore. Their first-round opponent in the NCAA Tournament, the Arizona Wildcats, was a nationally ranked powerhouse. The Wildcats were led by point guard Damon Stoudamire, a future NBA Rookie of the Year who would anchor the Toronto Raptors in their years as a fledgling expansion franchise. Stoudamire's back-court mate, Khalid Reeves, was a New York City high school legend later picked by the Miami Heat in the first round. And at forward the Wildcats started none other than Chris Mills, the Los Angeles high school standout who would become a first-round pick of the Cleveland Cavaliers and enjoy a ten-year career in the NBA. But for all that firepower, the Wildcats seemed unusually prone to upsets. A year earlier, as a No. 3 seed in the NCAA tourney, Arizona had lost out to East Tennessee State, a No. 14 seed, in the opening round. So when Nash and the 15th-seeded Broncos jumped out to a 33–21 lead against their No. 2–seeded foes, there was some expectation that the improbable could be possible. Only once before had a No. 15 seed defeated a No. 2, this back in 1991, when the Richmond Spiders had sent Syracuse home in a triumph of the underdog that no one had seen coming.

Still, when the Wildcats reeled off 25 unanswered points to snag a 13-point lead over Santa Clara, CBS, the tournament broadcaster, switched to another game. Seemingly incapable of missing from long range the previous weekend, Nash went 0-for-3 from three-point range in the Arizona game. But he made the first eight free throws he took. And though he could have been the game's goat after he missed two free throws in the dying seconds with Santa Clara ahead by 3 points, the misses proved inconsequential after a series of events that included a flubbed rebound by Mills, two more missed free throws by Santa Clara's Kevin Dunne, and the narrow miss of a three-pointer from the hand of Stoudamire that could have tied the game at the buzzer. Santa Clara ended the game on a 31–15 run to win 64–61.

"Don't take this the wrong way, but there's some luck involved in Steve's success," Woolery says. "Things have to fall in place. I remember a coach told me a long time ago, you have to be good to be lucky. And so, things happened. For example, he could have gone to another school, maybe a bigger school, and it wouldn't have worked out this way. For example, he could have played point and had success at point as a freshman. But with us going to the NCAA tournament . . . the announcers were excited to see Steve play because he had hit all these threes. Now, if he was just a good solid freshman point guard who averaged 6 points and 5 assists, nobody would have been talking about him at the NCAA tournament. But the fact was, he was 18 for 24 from three-point range in the previous eight games, or something like that—he had some lore. So that allowed him more opportunity and a bigger name."

In the summer between his freshman and sophomore seasons, Nash found more playing time at the point as part of a couple of national team efforts. He also got a harsh introduction to the perils of international competition. In a qualifying tournament for the world junior championship in Argentina, supporters of the host team pelted the Canadians with hot coins and chunks of ice originally intended for concession-stand drinks. Canada lost to Argentina and was blown out by 47 points against the United States, but there was a measure of redemption when Nash got back to North American soil.

Starting at point guard for the Canadian entry in the World University Games, Nash helped Canada put in a memorable effort in a gold-medal game against the Americans. The U.S. roster included future NBAers like Stoudamire of Arizona, another future Raptor, forward Carlos Rogers, and Nash's long-time teammate and friend in Dallas, Michael Finley. Such was their dominance that the Americans won their first six games by an average of 42 points. And yet, playing at Buffalo's Memorial Auditorium, a short drive from the border, the Canadians were hardly overwhelmed. They jumped out to a 25–9 lead in the first ten minutes and held on to end the half up 52–40.

Nash had already led his team to a 5–2 record in order to claim its spot in the gold-medal final. And after the U.S. pulled away in the second half, opening up a 10-point lead, Canada rallied and got within one with 2:48 left before the Americans finally closed them out 95–90.

"We had so many people telling us we had nothing to lose," Canadian coach Dave Nutbrown told the *New York Times*. "Well, then, there was no reason to play today. We already had the silver medal. We wanted to play for the gold. I was impressed that we didn't show any nervousness. There are professionals that can't do that."

The U.S. might have won gold, but the Canadians had made a bold enough statement of their own, and Nash, who had 13 points and 17 assists in the game, continued to grow his young legend. (During the games Nash and Stoudamire, whose Arizona Wildcats had suffered at the hands of Nash and his Santa Clara Broncos in the NCAA, finally met off the court. As the story goes, the two star point guards bumped into each other in an elevator at their Buffalo hotel. Stoudamire looked up at Nash and said, "I remember you.")

By his sophomore year he was wowing crowds with his swish-making heroics on a regular basis. In a game at the University of San Diego, he racked up 27 points and 6 assists. Hank Egan, the San Diego coach, was heard to marvel at Nash's knack for finding the bottom of the net.

"He made one from the parking lot, and we had someone on him," Egan said at the time. "He's a handful."

But despite his reputation as a feared designated shooter, Nash was, even then, a ball-sharing wizard at heart. As much as he spent long hours perfecting his jumpshot, his time at Santa Clara also saw him begin to perfect the array of passing options that would help make him one of the world's finest playmakers.

Among the weapons he continually worked on was the one-handed pass. The textbook, as written by the majority of the game's coaches, has usually frowned upon the use of only one hand in moving the ball from player to player. But as Nash went along in his college career, he became more and more predisposed to dishing out assists with the flick of a single wrist.

Magic Johnson was perhaps the most famous purveyor of the one-handed pass. To see the legendary Laker leading a fast break, his Showtime-era teammates filling the lanes, was to see a ball shared with laser-like economy. At times Johnson, 6-foot-9 with generously sized mitts, made it seem as though he was playing with a softball-sized basketball. Perhaps because Nash couldn't manipulate the ball with the same authority, his predilection for single-handed distribution disturbed his coach to no end.

"I said, 'Steve, goddamnit, you've got to quit throwing one-handed passes,'" Davey remembers. "I'm of the school, you throw two-handed passes. Even though he was successful with it, I'm telling him, 'You can't do it.'"

But Nash was never one to believe the orthodoxy. As a blanket statement, "Canadians don't become world-class players," was as close to the truth as "world-class players mostly take the time to wrap both hands around the ball before they send it in the direction of a teammate."

"Steve talked to me about it," Davey says. "He told me, 'When I penetrate, if I've got the ball in my left hand and I'm going to give it to a guy in the left corner while I'm in the lane, it's faster for me to throw it to him with one hand than it is to grab it with two and then throw it.' He said, 'I save [the shooter in the corner] about three-tenths of a second in his shot, so he's a little more open when he shoots it.' That's typical Steve."

There isn't a widely available stat to track such an advantage, although NBA teams have lately invested in ever more elaborate ways to measure the game's subtleties, including a system of overhead cameras that can track every movement made by every player in a game, down to the centimetre. The game's best players, though they'll take an open-minded glance at any data that's available, don't need a computer to tell them their instincts are on point.

"There's a certain amount of risk," Nash said years later. "If you take the time to gather with two hands, you're eliminating angles to deliver the ball and taking time away from a teammate to get a shot or an easy score. I'm always trying to maximize the opportunities to get a basket for me and my teammates."

That's not to say Davey became an advocate of teaching the one-handed pass to beginners. "I don't complain as much when guys do it now," Davey says. "But if you've got guys that do it and it hits the guy in the shoelace when you throw it to him—yeah, then I complain." And it's certainly not to say that the last two-hand purist has gone to his grave. In recent years Nate McMillan, the former Portland Trail Blazers coach, has been heard to chastise veteran pros for making one-handed passes. Then again, McMillan never coached Nash.

"I don't say he never threw a bad pass, because he made turnovers," says Davey. "But I'll tell you: almost every time he throws it to anybody, it's in a place where they can use it. And that's a big plus to a guy trying to score, that he gets it in a useable area. He gets it at the speed that he can receive it. If it's a longer pass, it's firmer. If it's a shorter pass, it's softer."

From freshman shooting sensation, Nash eventually emerged as a prototypical point guard. But in his sophomore year, when he was getting more minutes as Woolery's backup, he was still being referred to as "a poor man's Bobby Hurley"—a reference to the Duke University point guard who, for all his collegiate effectiveness, had a forgettable pro career following a serious car accident as a rookie.

By Nash's junior year, the comparisons had gone significantly upmarket. There were those who glimpsed Nash's numbers and admired his pass-first mentality and were reminded of another West Coast Conference point guard who'd already gone on to a stellar NBA existence, NBA All-Star John Stockton. The two did have certain things in common. Stockton was also white, for one. He was an unimposing 6-foot-3. He had come from off the radar, a smaller school called Gonzaga University in Spokane, Washington, to become a first-round NBA pick. Still, Stockton was half a career ahead of Nash. By the dawn of 1995, he was already a six-time NBA All-Star. He was in the midst of a streak that would see him lead the NBA in assists for nine straight seasons. And while Nash still wasn't impressing anyone with his defence, Stockton had topped the world's best league in steals in two separate seasons.

"To compare Steve Nash with John Stockton borders on the absurd," then Gonzaga coach Dan Fitzgerald, who coached Stockton, said in 1995, in the lead-up to Nash's senior season. "He certainly is a great player, don't get me wrong, but he's got one-fourth of his college career left to play. Is he a kid that you would think can make it? I think he has the competitive makeup to play in that league. I tell [scouts], 'You've got to take a real hard look.' I certainly think he can make it. But making it and being John Stockton—there's a little bit of a stretch there."

In hindsight, the stretch wasn't all that absurd. And even in 1995, Nash's collegiate resume looked awfully similar to Stockton's. Nash flirted with the prospect of leaving Santa Clara after his junior year to declare himself eligible for the NBA draft. After leading the conference in scoring and assists, he might well have been a first-round selection. But Nash decided to stick around.

It was a decision he'd already had to make more than once during his time there. By the end of his sophomore season, bigger-named programs had begun inquiring about his interest in transferring.

"I think there have been a couple of tampering situations, but I'm not going to worry about it," said Davey at the time. "If he wants to be here, I want him here. If he doesn't want to be here, he can go somewhere else. I realize we were lucky to get him."

Said Nash in 1995, "I finally decided that this school would provide me with the opportunity if I made the most of it. The NBA scouting network is so widespread that they're not going to miss players. And, of course, loyalty entered into it. They gave me a chance when nobody else did."

In Nash's senior year, he led the Broncos into the NCAA's Top 25 for their first time since 1972. He met Magic Johnson outside the arena at the Maui Invitational Tournament and watched the legendary floor general personalize an autograph, "Good luck from Big Magic to Little Magic." He heard Marty Blake, the NBA's director of scouting, make a pre-draft pronouncement that, four years earlier, would have seemed unfathomable: "Point guards like Nash are born, not made. He's going to have a long NBA career."

The high-schooler from Victoria who once felt like he was screaming in an elevator with no one around to hear him was suddenly en route to the penthouse suite with the basketball world at rapt attention. He'd be a first-round pick. He'd get the guaranteed millions that go with the privilege. But if he'd shown the scouts anything in his rise from unknown to all-American, it was that his greatest skill wasn't his dribbling or his passing or his shooting—it was his gift for going to work in the gym and getting a little bit better every day. Close observers took notice.

"You feel secure knowing that if Steve wins the lottery, he's not going to quit his job," is how Jim Hadnot, a New Jersey Nets scout, put it at the time. On the night in New York in June 1996 when the Phoenix Suns selected him fifteenth overall in the NBA's annual talent selection fest, Nash accomplished his young life's primary goal at age 22. "My holy grail," he'd called the NBA more than once, and now he was sipping from it. But if Nash deserved congratulations for a job well done, Hadnot was right: the Suns' new recruit was far from quitting. His life's work had only begun.

CHAPTER THREE

Dallas: The Making of a Rock-Star All-Star

I f Nash's NBA life began in Phoenix in the fall of 1996, when he commenced a two-season stint as a backup to Suns the likes of Jason Kidd and Kevin Johnson, he would enter his prime in Dallas a few years later. Dallas was the place Nash would emerge as an unquestioned NBA starter; it was the place he would find a basketball soulmate, Dirk Nowitzki, with whom he would sweat through the exhausting one-on-one games and exacting skill-development drills that would continue to elevate both their arsenals; it was the place where he would become an All-Star while developing into a unique locker-room presence for off-court views that were outside the mainstream. Dallas was also the place, in the lockout-shortened fifty-game season of 1999, where he would be mercilessly booed by frustrated home fans.

If you were to pinpoint the reason why Nash initially failed to win the hearts of the fans of the Dallas Mavericks, you'd do worse than to pinpoint this: that first season in

Texas, his jumpshot, which has since proven to be one of the most reliable in the history of the sport, would curiously abandon him. Coming to Dallas was a tremendous opportunity, but with the chance came considerable expectations. The Mavericks were possessed of a playoff drought that was eight seasons old when Nash was brought aboard as the unquestioned No. 1 point guard. And while the club's management saw tremendous promise in the recently assembled core that included Nash and a newly drafted seven-footer from Germany with a knack for three-point shooting, the presence of Nash and Nowitzki didn't pay immediate dividends.

It made fans in Dallas uneasy that the Mavericks had given up a first-round draft pick to acquire Nash (the pick would become Shawn Marion, the ninth-overall selection in 1999, who would star alongside Nash is his Suns heydey). It also didn't help that Dallas would win just nineteen games during the abbreviated schedule that followed Nash's trade. And it didn't exactly set the blood racing when assistant coach Donnie Nelson, son of Dallas head coach Don Nelson, would publicly acknowledge that the Mavs were a long way from finding the franchise player they'd been seeking. Also clouding matters was that in order to draft Nowitzki the Mavericks had passed on Paul Pierce, a more instant NBA success taken by the Boston Celtics. It wouldn't help, later on, that when Nash missed the final 10 games of his first season in Dallas with a recurring back strain, the Mavericks went a promising 5–5. Overall Nash's early struggles left Don Nelson defending the club's forfeit of its 1999 draft pick because a segment of Mavericks fans that thought the point guard in hand was less desirable than someone who hadn't played in the NBA yet. They had seen what they had and weren't all that impressed.

The same could be said about the public's sentiment toward NBA players at large during an ownership-imposed lockout that lopped thirty-two games off the 1998–99 schedule. Accustomed to arriving for training camps in October, players had found themselves out of work until January. They hadn't endeared themselves to the masses during the interruption. The *New York Times* had told the tale of woe of Boston Celtics point guard Kenny Anderson, who'd moaned about the necessity of selling select models from his fleet of eight luxury cars, this so he had "walking-around money" at a time when his exorbitant paycheques had failed to materialize. "I was thinking about selling one of my cars, I don't need all of them. You know, just get rid of the Mercedes," he said at the time, a joke that followed him throughout his career and beyond, as he declared bankruptcy despite earning $63 million during his thirteen years in the NBA. New York Knicks centre Patrick Ewing, meanwhile, had explained what he saw as the reality of the players' refusal to find quick accord in their financial dispute with owners: "We make a lot of money, but we spend a lot of money."

Nash was an unlikely target for fan disdain. He wasn't a lavish spender—he rented for most of his early NBA years; and his T-shirt and blue jeans wardrobe was far from flashy. But seen in the context of stories like Anderson's, perhaps it was a moment in sports history when signing a five-year contract worth $28.25 million, as Nash had just done, would breed a particular kind of backlash in the fan base, especially if a player's production wasn't up to par. Nash's contract wasn't the immediate source of fan angst, but he became a lightning rod for criticism soon enough. The negative emotions came to a boil in a game against the Houston Rockets in March of 1999. Nash, in that game and many others that season, couldn't find his shooting range. And while his sole purpose on the floor has never been to shoot and score, the threat of his jumpshot has always been key to setting up the other aspects of his skill set.

"For whatever reason, Stevie has been a great shooter his entire career. High school, college, with the Suns. And for whatever reason—maybe he lost his confidence, or he was going through the process of learning the point-guard position and maybe he wasn't looking for his shot as much as he should have—but his jumpshot took a hiatus," Donnie Nelson would recall years later. If he wasn't making shots, defenders didn't have to crowd him, and if they didn't have to crowd him it was harder for Nash to beat them off the dribble and set off the kind of defensive chaos he loved to exploit with his passing. He couldn't shoot and suddenly his game was as sturdy as a chair with three legs.

Perhaps his confidence was never lower than in that game against the Rockets. He missed his first seven shots, and not long after he hoisted his eighth—a three-pointer that also failed to connect—he was showered in the discontent of the fans at Reunion Arena. He was booed the next time he touched the ball, and almost every time he touched it thereafter. Nash first met the derision with a grin, but the blowback appeared to affect his approach to the game. He only attempted two shots in the second half. Even Charles Barkley, the Rockets forward who knew something about alienating a crowd, could sympathize. He offered Nash a consolatory pat on the derriere. "I'll face it with a smile on my face, and I'll be a winner one of these days," Nash would tell the *Dallas Morning News* days later.

Six years later, Nash would be standing at a microphone accepting his first of two MVP awards. He would be immortalized with a select list of repeat winners, from Michael Jordan to Magic Johnson to Larry Bird. Instead of consoling him, Barkley would be writing a tribute to him, extolling Nash as one of *Time* magazine's 100 people "Transforming the World." But at that moment, in the spring of 1999, it was difficult to see Nash and the Mavs as winners. Nash, in that hard-luck season, was suddenly a gimpy point guard shooting just 36.3 percent from the field in his thirty-one minutes of floor time.

"His first year in Dallas was as tough as it gets in basketball, period," Donnie Nelson says. "When you're a guy like Stevie, you're not born with Carl Lewis type speed, if you can't hit your outside jumpshot, it's death. Those incredibly athletic defenders you've got to face night in and night out, they can take a step off you. Now you can't get around 'em. And you don't have the confidence to shoot on 'em . . . People were lagging off him. He couldn't make a shot. It screwed with his confidence. It was really sad. It was very difficult, very emotional. Dirk wasn't playing worth a squat. These guys are both young and they're learning the positions. And Stevie went through, I think, a really gut-wrenching, very emotional time, kind of like Dirk did. But through the ashes of that, those two guys—that's where they became great."

It certainly wasn't the only time Nash would hear a home crowd boo his team. But this was different. This was a home crowd targeting the home team's point guard. Nash chose to meet the criticism head-on rather than turtle. "I understand fans have questions about me or there are some saying 'Who is this guy?' and that's okay," Nash told the Fort Worth *Star-Telegram* around the time he arrived in

Dallas. "I'm not promising I'll make the All-Star team because that can be political. But if I'm not playing at an All-Star level in three years, come to me because there won't be anybody else to blame." Coming from a player who hadn't yet convinced the basketball-loving masses of his elite potential, they were bold words. You didn't need to cast back very far into Nash's history to understand that even those who believed deeply in his potential didn't see his rise to an All-Star level as anything resembling an inevitability.

As NBA teams scouted talent for the 1996 draft, Nash's strong play in college had put him on a shortlist of the best available point guards. His was a position at which the Phoenix Suns, on the surface, didn't appear to need immediate help. Starter Kevin Johnson, a 30-year-old veteran, was a three-time All-Star. So it made sense that the Phoenix franchise had its eyes on talent at other spots on the floor. John Wallace, a gifted scoring forward from Syracuse University, was among the possibilities being discussed, as was a high school phenomenon from the Philadelphia area named Kobe Bryant.

"We had great interest in Kobe," Jerry Colangelo, the Phoenix franchise's patriarch, said. "We brought him to Phoenix. We worked him out. He was the real deal. And we were concerned about one possible thing happening, and it did. That was the Lakers making a deal."

Indeed, had the L.A. Lakers not made a franchise-altering trade that sent centre Vlade Divac to the Charlotte Hornets in return for Bryant, whom the Hornets agreed to draft with their thirteenth overall pick, Bryant might have become a Sun. As it was, Bryant became the cornerstone of five NBA championship teams in Los Angeles, where he would one day team with Nash in a late-career effort to squeeze out a couple more. The Suns, like every NBA team, held pre-draft meetings in which their brain trust mulled over the various scenarios that could unfold on draft day. But not everyone in the Phoenix hierarchy, not to mention the NBA at large, was convinced that Nash was worthy of the fifteenth-overall selection that the Suns possessed. Nash, in some corners, drew comparisons to John Stockton. But the less enamoured among the scouting community had compared him to Brent Price, the brother of All-Star point guard Mark Price, who despite carving out an NBA career that saw him play more than four hundred regular-season games, had never became an entrenched starter, let alone an All-Star.

"[Nash] was like a lot of smaller-school point guards. He knew how to play but the question was, 'How was that body going to withstand the NBA?'" said one California-based NBA scout. "You think back to that draft and you look at Allen Iverson and Stephon Marbury. I don't think anyone put Nash in the same conversation as those two."

Still, more than a few NBA voices went on record with glowing forecasts of Nash's future.

"You can see that," Bob Bass, then the GM of the Charlotte Hornets, said at the time of the Stockton-Nash comparison. "[Nash] likes to get in the middle of the defence and kick it outside to the open man. He's very good on the pick-and-rolls. There's some resemblance there. He's not as quick as John Stockton. He's probably as good a shooter as John is. He might be better before he gets through playing. I don't know if he can get to the basket [like Stockton]."

Nash, for his part, downplayed the comparisons to the former Gonzaga University star. He and Stockton had played in the same small Western college conference, but Nash was quick to point out the convenient superficiality of likening one relatively undersized, white point guard from that same conference to another.

"I think it's easy to put our names together," Nash was quoted as saying at the time. "But it's a little far-fetched since he's the all-time leader in assists and I haven't even played a game yet."

Donnie Nelson, then a Suns assistant coach, said that early in Phoenix's pre-draft talks, Nash "wasn't really in the conversation." But Nelson, as it turns out, had a better-than-average grasp on the range of Nash's potential. Donnie, a friend of Ken Shields, had known Nash since Nash was in high school. They first met when Shields arranged for Nash to attend a Golden State Warriors game against the Seattle Supersonics. The purpose of the trip was for Nash, who was slacking in the weight room at the time, to see powerfully built guards like the Warriors' Tim Hardaway and inspire Nash to work on his body as well as his game. But Nash also met the younger Nelson—his father, Don, was then head coach and general manager of the Warriors—and from there Donnie followed Nash fairly closely. He took note of him both in college and at the legendary pickup games at the College of Alameda, home to the Bay Area gym where the Golden State Warriors often held workouts and where Nash would frequently tangle with NBA-calibre competition while still enrolled at Santa Clara.

"We're in the job of projecting talents, and back then I thought he could be a starter in the NBA," Donnie

Nelson said. "I thought, at the very worst, he's going to be a heck of a backup coming off the bench."

Donnie Nelson shared his opinion with fellow assistant coach Danny Ainge who, as fate would have it, was a rising figure in the organization and would take over the position of head coach from Cotton Fitzsimmons eight games into the 1996–97 season. Soon Nash's name was being tossed around in Phoenix as a possible selection with the fifteenth pick.

"The night before the draft, Jerry [Colangelo] comes up to me. He says, 'Nellie, do you really feel good about this kid?' When Jerry comes and talks to you, it catches your attention when you're an assistant coach,'" Donnie Nelson said. "I've done this three times in my life. I'd just signed a long-term assistant-coach contract, like, a five-year deal. And I said, 'Jerry, if he's a failure, you can have my job. That's how [convinced] I am.' Sure enough, we drafted him."

The Stockton comparison got somewhat more apt when Nash arrived in Phoenix. The Suns, after all, already had a formidable starting point guard in Johnson. And not long after selecting Nash, they had acquired Sam Cassell, another promising point guard, only to flip Cassell to the Dallas Mavericks in a deal that brought them Jason Kidd, who would emerge as the best point guard in the NBA for the handful of years it took Nash to mature. Suddenly Nash, who'd been told by the Suns he was the franchise's point guard of the future, looked for the foreseeable future like the point guard of fourth-quarter garbage time. He started his rookie season buried on the bench as a third-stringer.

For Hall of Fame–bound ball handlers, it was not uncharted territory. Stockton, many forget, spent the bulk of his first three seasons with the Utah Jazz playing behind Rickey Green. The seemingly idle time riding the bench would later be viewed as an incubator of sorts. For players who work hard in practice and pay attention during games, being an NBA backup can be a peerless education. For Nash, mind you, the sitting wasn't easy. He had faced the same problem at Santa Clara. But while the solution there was to carve out a niche as a shooting guard, the NBA didn't provide the same latitude. The Suns had plenty of shooting guards, among them Wesley Person and Rex Chapman. They were bigger, stronger players with better credentials to man a position that generally demands a combination of size and explosiveness—two qualities Nash lacked.

"It's inevitable that everyone is going to look at that aspect of [the Kidd] trade [and] what it means to me," Nash said at the time. "I do a little. But for the most part, I just try to concentrate on getting better. I think if I concentrate on getting better my career will be successful regardless of where I'm playing."

That period on the Phoenix bench provided what Steve Konchalski—former Canadian national team coach, men's basketball coach at St. Francis Xavier University in tiny Antigonish, Nova Scotia, and winningest coach in CIS history—calls his favourite Steve Nash anecdote:

"I always followed my players and the second year I was coaching him with the national team was Steve's rookie year in the NBA and he was with Phoenix and they had Jason Kidd and Kevin Johnson at guard," says Konchalski. "It was February or March and I was touching base with all my players, wherever they were, and Steve was going through a stretch where he barely played. [After averaging a respectable 14.2 minutes a game in 41 appearances before the All-Star game that year, Nash averaged just 4.3 minutes a game in 24 appearances after the break.] So when I was calling him, I was a little bit reticent. I figured he'd be a little down or whatever because he wasn't playing.

"So I get him on the phone and ask him how he's doing and he says, 'I'm doing great, coach.' And after a little while I get around to asking him how he's handling not playing and he says, 'Listen, I have no problem with it. Practices are my games. I have the opportunity to play against two of the best guards in the NBA every day in practice and I have to get ready to practice against them like it's a game, every single practice. If I do that, I'm going to eventually get where I'm going to go.'

"How many players would take that attitude?" says Konchalski. "How many? To me there is no better barometer explaining how he got to where he got to. It's that attitude."

That, of course, was the only productive attitude to take. Nash's concentration on only what he could control served him well. Ainge, the Phoenix coach, said he "knew we had someone special" in Nash during the Canadian's rookie year; not from Nash's approximately ten minutes a game of court time, but from his practice habits. By the second half of his second year in Phoenix, opportunity had knocked enough to convince anyone who was paying attention that Phoenix's third-stringer was a first-tier talent. When Johnson needed surgery on a knee that would keep him out of the lineup for most of thirty-two games in the midst of Nash's sophomore year, Nash found minutes as a backup to Kidd. Johnson was off for all of December and January and Nash took the opportunity to simply go off—as much as a backup point guard can. In one six-game span during which he began to turn heads, he averaged more than 12 points a game and shot 60 percent from three-point range. For the two-month period Johnson was out Nash shot 44 percent from deep (which would have been good for No. 2 in the NBA over the entire season) and 49.1 percent from the floor overall while averaging an impressive 11.6 points a game off the bench. In a season that saw *USA Today* call him "the league's most coveted nonstarter," the buzz was building.

"He's better than half the starting point guards in the league right now," Ainge said. "The other day I was looking up and down NBA rosters. I found myself saying that Steve is better than this starter, better than that starter, and so on. Before long, I had eliminated half of the starting point guards in the league. I would not gamble on a deal for Nash. Hey, I love the guy."

This being the NBA, a player's value can turn on a dime. In June of 1998, after the Suns lost in the first round of the playoffs to the San Antonio Spurs, Nash was dealt to Dallas on draft day. Despite his coach's protests, the deal—which saw Nash swapped for a package that included players Pat Garrity, Martin Müürsepp and Bubba Wells, as well as the Mavericks' first-round pick—didn't set off widespread outrage in Phoenix. On the flip side, it didn't play all that well in Dallas. Never mind that while Garrity would become a productive if unspectacular contributor, the likes of Müürsepp and Wells never made NBA impact. Never mind that there were far worse draft-day dealings in the league that year (the Milwaukee Bucks, who swapped Garrity to Phoenix after they picked him nineteenth overall, also sent the Mavericks Nowitzki in exchange for the right to acquire Robert "Tractor" Traylor, whom the Mavericks had selected sixth overall in the draft. Traylor would become one of the biggest draft-day busts in NBA history, albeit in part because of a heart ailment that led to his 2011 death). At the time, dealing Steve Nash simply wasn't that big a deal.

The trade to Dallas wouldn't have happened without the influence of Donnie Nelson, who left Phoenix when his father landed the coach and GM post with the Mavericks in 1997, and who immediately pushed for Nash's acquisition.

"My dad was like, 'Well, how good do you think [Nash] can be?' At that point, the rest of the world really hadn't seen him. So I'm projecting off of him locking horns with Jason Kidd and Kevin Johnson in practice, and I told my dad, 'In your system, I think he can be a top-ten point guard in the NBA in assists,'" Donnie Nelson said. "That was a pretty big jump. My dad went through the same thing [Jerry] Colangelo did: 'Are you sure? . . . These are our balls that are on the line.'"

Both men's metaphorical privates stayed on that line a little longer than either was probably comfortable with. By the time the 1999 draft rolled around, Don Nelson found himself having to rationalize the decision to give up a first-round pick in the transaction that brought Nash to the Mavericks.

"We'd rather have Steve Nash than our pick," Don Nelson told Marc Stein, then of the *Dallas Morning News*. "We thought Nash would be better than any pick we could get, and I still believe that. Now he has to become the player I know he is. I don't know what else to tell you."

The organizational belief was heartening, given that Nash, in playing forty games in the lockout-shortened fifty-game schedule and averaging more than thirty-one minutes an outing, had managed just 7.9 points and 5.5 assists a game while shooting 36.3 percent from the field—hardly acceptable numbers for any respectable organization's unquestioned floor general. In fact, they were downright horrible—Nash became one of four players since the introduction of the three-point line in 1979–80 to shoot less than 37 percent from the floor while playing at least thirty minutes a night. This dubious distinction was more shocking still given that Nash was considered a good shooter and would go on to become one of the best shooters to ever play the sport. But then the Mavericks hadn't yet won back their long-lost respect as they suffered through a 19–31 record. All things considered, Nash may have been lucky that, outside of Dallas, no one was really paying attention.

Perhaps Nash's struggles, combined with his early-career bouts with various nagging injuries, had at least something to do with his not inconsiderable reputation for occasionally playing as hard off the court as he played on it. The tales of excess, to be fair, were mostly anecdotal and light-hearted. Mavericks equipment manager Al Whitley, one of Nash's childhood friends, once told *Sports Illustrated* of how Nash spearheaded a pre-training-camp bar crawl with a peculiar set of rules: the participants would only drink one beer at each bar, and they would run between bars. About six miles and an undisclosed number of brews later, Nash capped the exercise with a swim at a bar that happened to have an outdoor pool. Jörg Nowitzki, father of Dirk, marvelled at Nash's hardiness in an ale hall during one of Nash's semi-regular trips to the Nowitzki homestead in

Würzburg. "Germans can drink beer—but Canadians!" the elder Nowitzki enthused to *Toronto Star* sportswriter Chris Young, speaking of a 2001 off-season outing. "I think he drank about seven litres. He was boiled!"

If Nash was heroically boiled on European soil, back in Dallas he was a bachelor who still enjoyed an epic night out with friends. When it became obvious to him that he was famous enough that people were both recognizing and watching him, Nash was known to lead occasional forays to the city's gay clubs, where he and his cadre relished the scene and the relative anonymity. Nash's laddish lore includes the story of one such night, not long after the Sydney Olympics, on which he crossed paths with a Hollywood actress named Elizabeth Hurley.

"I'll confirm it was a gay bar and Elizabeth Hurley was there and we were there," said Andrew Mavis, one of Nash's teammates on the Canadian national squad. "But I won't comment on anything else."

In his brief flings with the boldface type of the celebrity-culture pages, Nash was often good for something a little more colourful than a staid "no comment." When his agent helped squash a rumour that Nash was romantically involved with Spice Girl Geri Halliwell, a U.K. tabloid concocted the headline "Geri Sunk by Slam-Dunk Hunk." When a British NBA TV show made reference to the story during an interview with Nash, he didn't flinch. "Oh, I've always been a slam-dunk hunk," he said.

"You just can't startle him," Mavericks teammate Loy Vaught once told the *Dallas Morning News*. "When you see Steve Nash, the first thing that pops into your head is, 'cool.' He's got that Clint Eastwood thing going. He talks kind of quiet with that raspy voice. He's never out of control."

On the court, of course, that wasn't always true. Don Nelson often spoke, somewhat admiringly, of Nash's wont to play "a little bit out of control and unpredictable." Still, in Dallas's competitive misery, there had to be accountability. Nash vowed to spend his summer "doing my work . . . to be a five-million-dollar point guard next year." Don Nelson, for his part, said he wanted Nash to shoot more, and set his bricklaying ways aside.

"He looks to pass too much, as far as I'm concerned," the coach said. "But he's a better defender than I thought. I think it will all work out."

It didn't work out immediately. Nash actually shot less during his second season in Dallas, wherein he was hampered by an ankle injury that cost him twenty-two games. And while he improved his shooting percentages from the field and from three-point range—going 47.7 percent and 40.3 percent, respectively—his assists declined. And the Mavericks, meanwhile, missed the playoffs for the tenth straight time, albeit while making a year-over-year improvement from eleventh to ninth place in the Western Conference standings.

As the Mavericks remained a competitive work in progress, Nash found a friend in Nowitzki. The pair had discovered early common ground in the subject of European soccer; during their first year in Dallas together, Nash invited Nowitzki, who was about four years his junior and living away from home for the first time, to his apartment to watch a match. Eventually they would rent units in the same complex. They would often drive to practices and games together. They would become, in the eyes of teammates, generally inseparable.

"They see each other, like, twenty hours a day," teammate Michael Finley joked with the press. "It's a little scary."

They were, in some ways, opposites—Nowitzki shy and quiet, Nash more outgoing and unflinching. But Nowitzki, like Nash, came from athletic stock. His father, Jörg, played high-level team handball in the former West Germany. His mother, Helga, was a member of the women's national basketball squad. His older sister, Silke, played the game internationally and professionally in the days before she became her brother's manager. And like Nash, Nowitzki was the subject of considerable scrutiny through the early hiccups in Dallas. Though he had been playing professionally in Europe since he was a teenager, he failed to immediately adjust to the speed of the NBA game. ("I can't believe how fast the guards are," he would say.) As he lumbered through a difficult rookie season, no end of pundits pointed out the apparent lack of wisdom in Dallas selecting Nowitzki in the draft instead of the still-available Pierce, the all-American forward from the University of Kansas who was acclimatizing just fine in Boston, eventually averaging 16.5 points a game and finishing third in voting for the league's Rookie of the Year. Nowitzki averaged just 8.2 points a game and shot a career-low 40.5 percent from the floor. Nash, who knew what it was like to have one's shortcomings chronicled even as you worked diligently to overcome them, could relate.

"You've got to believe their friendship was born out of the controversy surrounding them when they first came here," Donnie Nelson once said. "To go through the grinder like Steve and Dirk did, to be booed on your own court, to be called every name in the book and have your name dragged in the mud? How can two people not bond together when they were both under a microscope?"

Their therapy against basketball's cruel truths was to immerse themselves in more basketball. The Nash-Nowitzki habit of late-night training sessions would become the stuff of NBA legend. And their fearsome one-on-one battles satiated more than their obvious competitive hunger. If Don Nelson wanted more scoring, Nash needed to perfect a new arsenal of shots to make it easier to score regularly in the sweat-soaked midst of bigger men, so playing against Nowitzki helped him hone his fall-away jumpshot, his floater, and the array of in-tight lay-ins that allowed him to find the bucket from any angle. Nowitzki, in turn, needed more exposure to the über-quick reactions of an NBA-calibre little man—having Nash at his feet in those off-hours games offered a far better means of instant feedback than any drill a coach could design. So while Nash told interviewers that his friendship with Nowitzki was more important than basketball— "We'd be good friends if we met at the store, the library, or whatever"—it was undeniably rooted in a mutual bond with a game that doubled as a life's pursuit.

"There were a lot of rough times," Nash has said. "But we spent a lot of time in the gym, a lot of time talking each other through those early days. We were both new to the city; he was new to the country. I would have a bad game, or he would have a bad game, and we were just kind of there for each other."

As Nowitzki would say later, when the tough times had

passed and much success had washed over both men, "I don't know if I would be where I am if it were not for Steve."

The Mavericks didn't make the playoffs in Nash's first year with the team. And though they didn't make it the following year, either, that 1999–2000 campaign offered the first real promise that the Mavericks might be more than a perennial punching bag. The season was eventful in its own way. For one thing, it included a twelve-game cameo appearance from Dennis Rodman, the one-time great who was long removed from his early 1990s heyday, when he twice was named the NBA's defensive player of the year and led the league in rebounding on four separate occasions. But his presence on the roster came in the wake of an epochal ownership change.

In January of 2000, the Mavericks were purchased by Mark Cuban, an Internet billionaire who would become one of the most controversial figures in the NBA's coming decade. Cuban paid real estate mogul Ross Perot Jr. about $280 million for a majority stake in the team. In the ensuing years Cuban would become famous as a jersey-wearing courtside presence who would rack up hundreds of thousands of dollars in fines for criticizing referees. But Cuban's impact on the team's fortunes would be nearly immediate. He began to spend lavishly on everything from the team's payroll to its coaching staff; at one point in his early years, the Mavericks would employ nearly one coach for every player. Cuban installed high-definition TV screens in every player's locker, complete with a Sony PlayStation, a DVD player and a VHS tape player for either analyzing game film or relaxing with a pre-game movie. He fed players with in-arena buffets that would later become a league standard (and generally limit the necessity of fast-food runs to fuel the league's multi-million-dollar investments).

And though the coaching staff assumed they would be relegated to the dustbin by this new owner who was so clearly looking to put his stamp on the operation—upon receiving word of Cuban's acquisition of the team, Don Nelson took his assistants out to eat for a meal that was immediately coined "The Last Supper" by the staff—it wouldn't be long before Cuban signed Nelson to a contract extension that ran more than a decade. Again defying convention, when Cuban signed Rodman, he invited the NBA's foremost purveyor of extreme body art and feather boas to stay in his home.

"I am gonna have a blast," Cuban said at the time. "Everybody dreams about what they'd do if they won the lottery. Well, this is it for me, owning a team I really care about."

Cuban's story was its own American wonder. Some four years after he and a friend co-founded Broadcast.com, a pioneering Internet radio and TV site they'd originally conceived as a way to listen to Indiana University men's basketball games when they weren't within reach of the Hoosier state's airwaves, Cuban and his partner sold the company to Yahoo! for about $6 billion. That vaulted Cuban to No. 28 on the Forbes list of richest Americans. The Pittsburgh-bred son of an automobile upholsterer father, Cuban bought a $40 million private jet and a 24,000- square-foot mansion worth about $16 million. If some fans would come to cringe at Cuban's bombastic presence—he frequently opined about the state of all things in interviews, in emails to media members, and on his blog—they couldn't deny his outward passion for the game. Dallas's previous owner acknowledged he knew little about the game aside from the fact that a typical basket is worth two points, and perhaps it was no coincidence that under Ross Perot Jr., the Mavericks had played as though the boss didn't know the difference between good basketball and bad. The Mavericks, to wit, compiled an abysmal .295 winning percentage under Perot's ownership. Cuban, at least, was a sincere and passionate supporter of the team who had been a frequent presence at Mavericks games long before he owned the team. He'd been a part of the so-called "Reunion Rowdies"— a group of hard-core supporters who were known to be the life of Reunion Arena, the team's home until the completion of American Airlines Center in 2001. The story goes that Cuban, who as a bachelor lived in a three-bedroom apartment he shared with five other friends, didn't attend the team's late-1980s playoff games because post-season ticket-price increases made them prohibitive. But things began to look up for the budding entrepreneur in 1990, when at 34 years of age he sold a computer company he founded for $6 million. And it was only a handful of years later, after Broadcast.com became one of the great success stories of the Internet boom, that Cuban wasn't merely sitting in courtside seats he could have never previously afforded—he was pondering a sea change in the team's fortunes, both competitive and financial. Cuban, from the beginning, made profits a secondary concern.

"There's winning and then there's everything else," he said at the time. "I'll do everything in my power—financially and with sweat equity—to make this team a champion. I won't accept anything less."

———

Winning did not come easily for the Mavericks or for Nash. If Nash's first year in Dallas had been marked by the grumpy furor of fans who occasionally took out their frustration on the home team, word would later get out that he'd been nursing a nasty case of plantar fasciitis. The painful condition, an inflammation of the tissue that runs along the bottom of the foot, helped explain why he struggled so mightily both as a shooter and as a playmaker. His follow-up season wasn't much better—and again, injury was an issue. A strained ligament in his ankle kept him out of about 30 percent of his team's schedule; in the end, he played just fifty-six games and started only twenty-seven of them. In the coming thirteen seasons, never again would Nash play in an NBA game in which he wasn't a starter; but, for now, it was all patience, hard work and an eye on the future.

A turnaround was in the offing in Dallas. And though it began to take shape at the tail end of the 1999–2000 season, when the Mavericks won nine of their final ten games, it didn't draw much attention until 2000–01. That season, the Mavericks inscribed a bold message on their media guide: "It's Payback Time." It was a warning to the NBA bullies who'd beaten up on the hapless Mavs of old: this was a different, more formidable Dallas squad. Nowitzki, who would average more than 20 points a game for the first of many times in his career, emerged as a go-to scorer who could take the pressure off of shooting guard Michael Finley. ("I finally have some help," Finley would say.) Nash, meanwhile, characterized himself as a "different player" than the injury-ravaged one who had laboured through his first two seasons with the club. He was healthy. He was playing more aggressively. That he averaged career highs in both points (15.6 a game) and assists (7.3) was hardly happenstance. It was just the start. In 2001–02 the Mavericks led the NBA in scoring, a title a Steve Nash–led team held for eight of the next nine seasons.

"We told him the past two years, 'You are a great shooter—shoot it,'" Donnie Nelson said. "When Steve is making his outside shot, it opens up the drives inside. An opponent has to decide, do you give him the open shot, or do you let him penetrate? I can't answer that question, and I coach him."

Nash finished third in balloting for the league's most improved player award that season. Certainly he possessed one of the league's most improved images. No longer a target for the ire of the Reunion Rowdies, Nash was at the centre of an enviable renaissance that saw the Mavericks win fifty-three games en route to their first playoff berth in eleven years.

"We went from having a half-filled arena at the start of the year to having it full every night," Nash said. "That transformation has been fun to be a part of. We've created a lot of excitement and the fans have created a lot of excitement back for us."

The excitement, once the playoffs began, seemed like it wouldn't be sustained for long. Dallas's opponent was the vaunted Utah Jazz, a franchise embarking on its eighteenth straight post-season run. The Jazz were anchored by power forward Karl Malone and by Stockton, both of whom had long established themselves as elite performers. Even though both were in their late thirties, they remained formidable competitors who were only a few years removed from back-to-back trips to the NBA Finals, where they twice were thwarted by none less than Michael Jordan's Chicago Bulls. When the Jazz won the first two games of their best-of-five series with the Mavericks in Salt Lake City, few people were surprised.

But the Mavericks were not finished. Returning home, they mounted a memorable charge. Nash was at the centre of a victory in Game 3 that saw his skin slashed open in a teeth-to-forehead collision with Stockton. Even with a brown bandage stuck to his forehead to protect a cut that required seven in-game stitches, Nash scored the winning basket with twenty-two seconds remaining in regulation time—a spinning nine-foot bank shot that forced another must-win contest.

"I'm hoping this scars, so I can have a memento," Nash told reporters of the trauma above his brow.

Nash was otherwise deferential in describing his tête-à-tête with Stockton, who at the time was already the NBA's all-time leader in assists and steals.

"He's one of the best point guards ever," Nash told reporters. "To play against him is a great experience and a lesson."

Certainly Don Nelson, a veteran coach, wasn't going to give the Jazz bulletin-board material from which to draw inspiration.

"I don't think anyone is trying to say [Nash is] better than John Stockton," the coach said. "But Steve sure is battling. Maybe by the time Stockton is forty or forty-five, he'll be better."

The truth was that Nash was doing just fine against Stockton. The Canadian scored 27 points (to Stockton's 4) in

Game 4, which Dallas won in a blowout, 107–77. And suddenly the Mavericks were on the verge of their second renaissance in one season. In the year when they ended a decade-plus playoff drought, they were also coming back from the post-season dead. In the decisive Game 5, there were moments when it looked bleak. With the Mavericks down 14 points heading into the fourth quarter, Nash had been held scoreless. But both he and his team rallied when it counted. Nash hit a trio of three-pointers in the final frame to aid in yet another headline-making comeback.

"It was make a few shots or go home for the summer," Nash said. "Michael [Finley, who had 33 points in Game 5] kept us hanging around for so long, the least I could do was make a couple . . . We kept our composure. A lot of times we could have folded, but we hung in there, and now we're going on."

Dallas became just the sixth team in NBA history to face a 2–0 series deficit and win the best-of-five set. In doing so the team carved out a niche as a scrappy squad that played with reckless abandon. "They like to play street basketball," Charles Barkley said of the Mavericks in one of his first forays as a TV analyst.

"All you people in Dallas, I hope you're partying, because that's exactly what I'm going to do," Cuban said after the unlikely comeback. "Y'all have a cocktail for me and on me."

The party was short-lived. Beating the Jazz gifted the Mavericks the privilege of being matched against the San Antonio Spurs in the next round. Heading into the best-of-seven series, the Spurs had defeated Dallas in thirty-nine of their forty-nine most recent meetings and were only a season removed from their 1998–99 NBA championship. A franchise led by a front line that included a pair of elite big men in Tim Duncan and David Robinson, their foundation rested on a vaunted defensive discipline that was known for turning the best offences into dysfunctional messes. Only one team in the NBA, the New York Knicks, had a better defence as measured by opponents' field-goal percentage. And the Spurs led the league in defending the three-point shot during the regular season. Perhaps not surprisingly, San Antonio won the first three games of the series before Dallas managed a token win of their own. In all, San Antonio's four victories over the Mavericks came by an average of more than 15 points a game.

So a rising team had work to do to achieve its outsized goals. But for Nash, as much as there was satisfaction in the progress, there was also beauty in the journey. As much as Dallas's elevation from doormat to playoff team was significant—this was professional basketball, after all, and winning paid the bills—perhaps just as significant for Nash was the revelation that he could win and not lose sight of the bigger picture in the process. Navigating the contradictions of a big-dog-eats-all culture was no easy feat, and in 2001 Nash opened up about his approach to the terrain.

"I want to win, but it's important not to hold onto something too tightly," Nash told the *Salt Lake Tribune*. "If you want something too badly, you might choke it. So I try to relax and have fun so I can play the best I can. I just want to be a happy person. I want to focus on the positive—in my own life and in the lives of others . . . People are important to me. I don't want to waste my existence concerned solely with myself. I want to be happy and make others happy.

I guess I just want to be nice to people around me. That's a much greater way to live your life. Negativity, in all of its forms, is a useless device. As much as possible, I want to eliminate negative energy from my life and the lives of others. I'd like to help others grow, and then, feel better about myself as well. I'm not religious in the contemporary sense. I don't know all the answers, but I don't worry about needing all the answers. I'm just an optimist."

Nice guys needn't finish last, apparently. Because for all the work Nash was doing to become the player and person he wanted to be, circumstances were playing their part as well. It became a little easier to be an optimist about a small man's role in the NBA in the season that followed Dallas's long-sought reintroduction to playoff competition. The 2001–02 season saw the NBA implement a handful of rule changes designed to improve the flow and increase the pace of the game. Jerry Colangelo headed the committee that suggested the changes, among them the scrapping of the league's complicated illegal defence rules. And though many players at first were skeptical of the wisdom of the shift— Shaquille O'Neal called the new rules "idiotic" and "stupid" and mused about retiring if the league didn't make a prompt return to the status quo—hindsight suggests the adjustments went some way toward opening up the middle of the floor to penetration by eye-pleasing ball-handlers like Nash.

"I went to [commissioner] David Stern and I said, 'David, right now I'm a little turned off with the way the game looks.' Scoring was down. Shooting was down. There was a lot of mugging in the paint. The guidelines for illegal defence, nobody understood. There were a lot of things that needed to happen," Jerry Colangelo said. "[Stern] said,

'Go ahead. Make a committee and do what needs to be done.' The result of that committee, we quickened the game up, went from ten seconds to eight seconds to advance the ball. We eliminated the defensive guidelines [and allowed zone defence]. We cleaned up the action in the middle [by making it a violation for defenders to stand in the lane in excess of three seconds at a time]. And by the way, all of these things led to more scoring, better shooting, a cleaner game, no isolation in the game. And it gave the little guy a chance to come back in the game and be really important."

The post-season would hold disappointment for Dallas in the future. They would lose again in the second round in 2001–02 before making a run to the Western Conference final in 2002–03. But through those years, while the Mavericks emerged as one of the league's highest-scoring teams, Nash pushed his game to new levels of production. In the early part of 2001–02, Nelson had threatened conse-quences if Nash didn't assert himself more aggressively on the offensive end—"shoot more or you'll be sitting," was the gist of the coach's prodding—and Nash, though defer-ential by nature, saw the benefits of increasing his fre-quency of attack through the NBA's painted area.

The lessons of Nash's first year in Dallas were hammered home as the Mavericks began to climb the league's ranks. As Nash figured out more ways to score with efficiency, he found his assist totals didn't suffer. In the season that ended in the spring of 2002, Nash averaged 17.9 points a game while also racking up 7.7 assists a game; both were career highs, as was his 45.5 percent shooting from three-point range, which was fifth-best in the league and first among point guards. Perhaps to no one's surprise, those kinds of numbers helped land Nash a spot on the Western Conference's roster at the NBA All-Star Game, his first of eight such nods. It was a monumental achievement, to be sure; no Canadian had ever before been able to call himself an NBA All-Star.

"I can't see any point guard in the West playing better," Gregg Popovich, the San Antonio Spurs coach, said at the time.

"[Nash] had total control of the game," added Milwaukee coach George Karl in the wake of a loss to the Mavericks.

Indeed, at the time he was named to his first All-Star squad, he was averaging 19.3 points and 8.0 assists a game—both career high-water marks. By shooting 49.5 percent from the field, 44.4 percent from three-point range and 88 percent from the free-throw line he found himself among the top 16 in the league in each discipline.

"His hair says it all. It's Steve's way of saying that although he is an NBA All-Star, there is more to him than his stats on the court," Cuban said in 2002.

Indeed, Nash's varying hairstyles had drawn nearly as much attention as his improving play. His look had been likened to that of an impoverished beach bum and a poor man's David Bowie.

"He looks more like a rock star than a basketball player," NBA coach Doc Rivers once observed.

"He defines himself as an individual with his own ideas and goals," Cuban said. "There probably isn't a topic Steve couldn't have an intelligent conversation about, which makes being around him a lot of fun."

The more Nash prospered at the point, the more people wanted to know about the man beneath the oft-unruly mop. There would be other on-court high points in Dallas. The Mavericks would sweep a first-round playoff series over Minnesota in 2002 before they were stopped cold, four games to one, by the Sacramento Kings. A year later Nash would quarterback them on their longest playoff run yet—a trip to the Western Conference final, where they'd lose in six games to the San Antonio Spurs and their twin giants, Robinson and Duncan.

Still, doubts about Nash's health began to creep into the team's long-range planning. Dallas had made a blockbuster trade-deadline deal in 2002 that fetched a handful of players, among them Nick Van Exel, who only further crowded a point-guard depth chart that at the time also included Avery Johnson. There was a concern that Nash, who was suffering through a strained right Achilles tendon at the time, was too hard on his body to be a bedrock player.

"He plays like a dervish, darting, weaving—and falling. His floor burns have floor burns," the great *Sports Illustrated* scribe Jack McCallum wrote at the time.

The Mavericks lost in the first round of the 2004 playoffs in what was a rare moment of underachievement for a team that had been on the upswing. Nash's contract was up, and so was his stock. Booed by the home fans five scant years ago, he had transformed himself into a local hero, an established member of the elite in the world's best basketball league. Dallas was the place where Nash made his NBA bona fides. Dallas was, in so many ways, home. But in the unsentimental world of pro sports, the place that gave him a shot to be a star would soon be selling him short.

CHAPTER FOUR

From Middle Seat to Pilot's Chair on the National Team

I t was five days in August 2012, but it felt like the future, and Nash, forever expert at seeing things before they unfolded for everyone else, was at the centre of it. For once he was where he always talked about being: at the Air Canada Centre in Toronto, in the Raptors' practice facility, playing basketball. But the wrinkle was that he wasn't there as a member of Canada's only NBA club — a possibility he'd entertained as a late-career landing spot as far back as his first kick at free agency in Dallas, and would again most seriously prior to signing with Los Angeles in the summer of 2012. He wasn't even there — officially, at least — as a player. Instead, Nash was shooting hoops as a unique hybrid: the new general manager of his favourite team of all — Canada Basketball's senior men's national team — and also a living, sweating, pick-and-roll-running pied piper to a collection of the best basketball players the country has ever produced, not to mention a shining example of human possibility many of those in the gym had looked up to ever since they'd first touched a ball.

Those on the floor took notice. A group of twenty-something ballers aren't going to start shrieking like their little sisters might meeting Justin Bieber, but there was a breathless, "I-can't-believe-this-is-happening-to-me" subtext for some as they recounted their summer camp stories. Take Kevin Pangos, for example. The star point guard for Gonzaga University was born in 1993 and grew up in Holland Landing, a small community north of Toronto where his mother was a gym teacher and his father the women's basketball coach at nearby York University. You could make the case his whole basketball life has been shaped by Nash's presence in his imagination. Pangos has never had a conscious thought about his basketball future without Nash figuring in as a glowing sunrise, promising that anything is possible for a Canadian kid with talent, dreams and a work ethic to match. With his short brown hair and boyish looks, "clean cut" is a description that attaches itself to Pangos like a middle name. But as a youngster, when he was first getting serious about basketball, his hair was long and floppy, in a tribute to a certain Canadian NBA star with a slacker style. "I wanted to be Steve Nash," said Pangos to the local press. "I look at a lot of point guards and try to learn from their game, but a guy like Steve Nash, he's my size, we have similar athletic ability so I just always try to learn from him. I'm trying to put my career along that path."

And now, here he was in the Raptors' gym, getting ready to practice with and against the man himself. The occasion was the first of what Nash hopes will be regular get-togethers with a rapidly expanding pool of Canadian basketball talent, and Nash's first opportunity to put a public stamp on what Canada Basketball could look like under his watch.

Nash had been announced as the general manager of the men's program that had been so much a part of his own development back on May 8, 2012. As always, his sense of timing was flawless.

"Hopefully—not to diminish my passion for the country and the sport—but I feel like now's the time to capitalize, not just because of the immediate success we can have, [but the] impact [we can have on] the kids to go to the highest level they can," said Nash when he was introduced alongside former national teammate and close friend Rowan Barrett, who will be the team's assistant general manager.

"If we can do that," Nash continued, "if we're successful converting as much of this talent from the NBA to Olympic quality basketball players, we can inspire the next generation, and we can change the game for the better at this point. I think it's really important to ignite that next generation."

For Wayne Parrish, the CEO of Canada Basketball, the mission as Nash described it said much about the new general manager himself: "He's going to be a lighthouse for all the great Canadian players coming up."

But what would a program run to the specifications of Canada's only basketball superstar—and one with a full-time job at that—actually look like?

The five-day training camp in August was a glimpse, and it looked great. The gym was filled with thirty-three players and twenty coaches wearing red and white. They represented both the current wave of national team talent— a group short on recent international success—and a strong contingent of the next wave, players for whom the national team was one choice among many available paths to fulfill their basketball hopes.

It was a big statement for a perennially cash-strapped national sports organization to make—to fly in, feed and put up three teams' worth of players and a classroom full of coaches, even though there were no games to be played and no competition to train for. But it was a sign that times were changing. And it resonated all the more loudly because the guy who brought it together was still the best player on the floor.

For those who'd never had the pleasure of playing with Nash—which was pretty much everyone given he'd last played for Canada in 2003—it was like seeing the statue of David step down and start dribbling behind his back and whipping no-look passes at unsuspecting tourists.

"I wasn't nervous, it was pure excitement for me," says Pangos. "It was just a chance to see how he does things, the way he moves. He's so smooth on the court, he's so efficient with how he gets it done. It was really neat.

"We were doing ball-handling drills the first day and we were going through cones as pretend defenders and I followed him and he said, 'No, you can go ahead' and I was like, 'No, no, no. You go first and I'm going to watch you and I'll try and do what you do.' I tried, didn't do it quite as well. He was so smooth and efficient. It's something I'll take with me throughout the year until I get a chance to work with him again. It's perfect. I couldn't have asked for a better [camp]."

Pangos wasn't the only Nash admirer on the floor.

Myck Kabongo couldn't have come from a background

more different than the semi-rural comfort Pangos knew. His family immigrated to Toronto from Zaire and he grew up on the rough edges of the city's downtown core. But the speedy point guard from the University of Texas held one example above all others when he was making his way through the U.S. high school system: Steve Nash.

"I've looked up to him my whole life," says Kabongo. "He changed basketball really, he made it cool to play up and down. For someone to accomplish what he has at his size, as a Canadian, from a hockey country, he's a Canadian hero."

The hero got cut. In the summer of 1991, Nash wasn't yet the greatest basketball player ever to carry a Canadian passport. He was a 17-year-old who was well known in Victoria and gaining recognition in British Columbia, but hardly anyone's choice to be the guy who would influence generations of players that would come after him. He was coming off a year in which he hadn't even played high school basketball, having had to sit out a season after transferring schools. He was in his "trapped in an elevator" phase, being recruited by exactly zero NCA Division I schools. Most pressing, he wasn't the choice of Ken Olynyk, who was the head coach of Canada's junior national team. It was a big summer for Olynyk. He'd been preparing Canada's best junior players for three summers in advance of the World Championships, which would be held in Edmonton that year. The arrival of Nash at the selection camp was interesting, but there were no thunderbolts to signal something really important was happening.

"I had been told he was really good," says Olynyk, who is now the athletic director of Thompson Rivers University in scenic Kamloops, B.C., but now better known now as the father of Kelly Olynyk, the first-team all-American centre and national team player who starred at Gonzaga alongside Pangos. "But I hadn't seen him play in high school and when he came into camp I thought he was really solid."

Nash came into the camp hopeful, but not expectant. He was still finishing Grade 11, for one thing, while a good chunk of the team was made up of older players like Barrett, the highly touted star of what was then a much-hyped Toronto high school scene. Barrett was wrapping up his fifth and final year of high school and heading to St. John's University in New York City. At his position Nash was fighting for a spot against guys like Sherman Hamilton, another Toronto-area star who was heading to Virginia Commonwealth University, or John Ryan, a technically sound, older and more experienced guard who came from tiny Sussex, New Brunswick.

"Some of those guys were like men," says Nash, with the benefit of twenty years of hindsight. "They were nineteen and I was seventeen. Even guys who didn't stick around the national team program were physically more dominant. When you go on and become a good college player and play in the NBA, everyone looks back and is like, 'I can't believe Olynyk cut him,' but at the time I probably wasn't ready."

Those who were at the camp remember Nash being a good player, but he didn't leave a searing impression.

"I just remember he would never, ever get tired," says

Hamilton, who would go on to become Nash's long-time national team backcourt partner and friend. "We used to run trails at the University of Lethbridge and we had some guys on that team who were pretty good long distance runners and they couldn't touch him. Steve would never, ever get tired. Never.

But on the court Nash was just another guy to beat. "In practice we had some battles. He wouldn't give up and I wouldn't give up, we were going for the same minutes. But was I surprised he didn't make that team? I couldn't have cared less. Could not have cared less," says Hamilton. "Back then I'm trying to make a name for myself and establish myself as a player in the program for future years. I didn't really care about who wasn't there. All I know was, I was on the team so I had to make a mark."

Still, being the coach who cut Steve Nash isn't necessarily the greatest bullet point to have on your resume. That's part of the reason more than twenty years later Olynyk can still recall the reasoning that went into the decision.

"We were going to be centralizing for May and June, which meant it was going to be difficult for him to stay and complete school, so he was made an alternate, and when I let him go, I told him if something happens I'd look at making a change," says Olynyk. "It was tough because he wasn't better than the guys we had, I thought. And he was younger. The guys from Ontario were finishing Grade 13 and going to university, and Steve had just finished Grade 11 and was going back to high school.

"That's how I justified it. But that might have all been a way for me to appease myself as much as it was the right decision."

Still, Nash participated in the team training as an alternate right until the tournament started in late July. Long enough, it turned out, to make his mark.

"Long Beach State came up and played six games against us and he was really, really good in one of those games," says Olynyk, wistfully. "He was six-for-six from the field, he had nine assists and I was just like—oh my God, this guy is going to be really good."

It wasn't a lost summer for Nash. As it turns out, it was those games against Long Beach State that helped him get his scholarship, because it was an assistant coach there who alerted the staff at Santa Clara to his potential. So will Nash be calling out Olynyk at his Hall of Fame induction speech, the way Michael Jordan famously reserved a few choice words for Clifton Herring, the coach who relegated him to junior varsity when he was in Grade 10 and forever became known as "the guy who cut Michael Jordan"?

"Those guys had been on the radar for a while," says Nash. "I never took it as a slight. I took it as, 'This is my obstacle and now I have to get over that hump.'

"Others might hold it against Ken, but I don't hold it against him. I was an alternate and I never really thought twice about it."

And then Nash smiles, a twinkle in his eyes: "I always liked Ken."

That one national team setback was a rare blip.

His dominant performance at the 1993 World University Games in Buffalo became a sort of coming-out moment for Nash. Leading a squad made primarily of Canadian university players, he proved the kind of impact he could have even among elite competition as he finished the gold medal game with 11 points and a stunning 17 assists—an unusually high total in a forty-minute international contest.

There's no question that playing for Canada meant something very special to a kid raised on the exploits of Team Canada hockey and the stirring passion of World Cup soccer. If his true gift is finding the elixir that brings out the best in his teammates, then playing for his country was something akin to the perfect laboratory environment. Absent the financial undercurrent that throbs through an NBA dressing room, basketball was once again a place to play and compete with friends for a shared goal.

"I've had an incredible time playing with the Canadian team—learned a lot, grown a lot, enjoyed my teammates and coaches more than anything," he said when he was considering retiring from the program. "I grew up in Canada, and those are very impressionable and formative years. They are very fond memories, and I developed such a closeness with the guys on those teams and my country that it's a very important part of my life."

Looking back, what's interesting about Nash's senior national team years is that—objectively at least—they lacked a signature moment or achievement. The acknowledged high point was the 2000 Olympics in Sydney, when Nash led Canada to a seventh-place finish. (There was also a seventh-place finish at the World Championships that Canada hosted in 1994.) And there was at least one perceived low point—a twelfth-place finish at the World Championships in 1998, a summer of competition that

Nash missed because NBA players were barred from the competition due to the NBA lockout.

Against some high-octane international opponents, Nash and his peers were setting high standards for themselves, but they weren't necessarily breaking new ground. Beginning with the 1974 World Championships and carrying through to the 1988 Summer Olympics, Canada was something of a world power—if you use the definition loosely. Their worst result at a major competition was eighth at the Worlds in 1974. Under the hand of the late Jack Donohue, the wonderfully accented New York City native who coached Kareem Abdul-Jabbar in high school and was Canada's first—and last—full-time head coach for the national team program, Canada finished fourth at home at the 1976 Olympics in Montreal, getting blown out 95–77 by the U.S. in the semi-finals. In 1978, Canada sent a young team to the World Championships in the Philippines and finished sixth, led by the country's first basketball prodigy. An 18-year-old Leo Rautins—having just graduated from high school—averaged 19.7 points a game as Canada looked to be a team on the rise, losing to the U.S. by 6 points in preliminary competition and by two in a classification game.

Many people still believe the strongest national team Canada ever assembled would have been Basketball Canada's entry for the 1980 Olympics, had Canada not ultimately boycotted the games (they were held in Moscow at the height of the Cold War). Further evidence of Canada's international strength long before Nash and his contemporaries took to the court includes another sixth-place finish at the 1982 Worlds and a gold medal at the 1983 World University Games in Edmonton (where Canada knocked off a U.S. team featuring Hall of Famers Charles Barkley and Karl Malone in the semi-finals and Yugoslavia in the finals). Canada finished fourth at the 1984 Olympics, a result tainted by the Eastern Bloc boycott, and wound down an era of consistent success with a sixth-place finish at the 1988 Olympics in Seoul.

But those were high points that for a decade Canada seemed unlikely to approach again. Donohue retired after the 1988 Games, as did stalwarts like Pasquale and future NBA coach Jay Triano. Ken Shields was appointed head coach and his technocratic ways chafed at some of the veteran pros recruited to help Canada qualify for the 1992 Olympics. They lost to the Dream Team 105–61 in the Tournament of the Americas in Portland, faring about as well as anyone else did in the summer of 1992. Canada eventually finished fifth in the tournament and didn't make it to Barcelona.

That the Dream Team had even been formed was proof that the basketball world was changing. In thirty-six years of Olympic competition, the United States had lost just once, to Russia in the controversial gold medal final at the 1972 Games; this while sending college players to compete internationally against teams of veteran European pros or—in the case of the Eastern Bloc countries—players who played full-time on behalf of the state. But the gap had been closing. In 1988, a team anchored by eventual Hall of Famer David Robinson could do no better than third at the Olympics. "It was a disgrace," Robinson said later. "We shamed our country." The year before Seoul, in the finals of the 1987 Pan American Games in Indianapolis, the U.S. had been torched by Brazil's Oscar Schmidt to the tune of

46 points, as the Americans lost a game on home soil for the first time. Further proof came in 1990 when a team of U.S. college players could do no better than bronze at the World Championships.

The 1992 Olympic Games were an accelerant. The U.S. romped to gold, yes, but also fired the imaginations of some very talented young athletes. Some of Nash's best professional moments would come in Dallas alongside Dirk Nowitzki, a 14-year-old in 1992 who was just getting serious about the sport at that point in tiny Würzburg, Germany. Pau Gasol, Nash's current teammate with the Los Angeles Lakers, was a 12-year-old in Spain. Both were captivated by the Dream Team and together they became perhaps the best international players in NBA history. Twelve years later, a team of NBA professionals could do no better than bronze at the 2004 Games in Athens and again at the 2006 World Championships—results that turned U.S. Basketball on its head.

The timing of the world's surge forward in international basketball couldn't have been worse for Canada. Bogged down in a slumping economy, hungover from the buildup to the 1988 Winter Games in Calgary and stinging still from the Ben Johnson doping scandal, Canada was entering an austerity period in its commitment to national sports organizations.

In that cash-strapped context, Nash's years with the national team are all the more impressive. When he famously dug into his own pocket so his teammates could have some spending money during the buildup to the 2000 Olympic Games in Sydney, what his generosity obscured was the need for him, or someone, to do it. Canada Basketball had been operating on a threadbare budget for years, with training camps shortened and travel and accommodations done on the cheap at every turn.

By the time Wayne Parrish took over as the chief executive director in the summer of 2007 it was an organization effectively under water.

Parrish found himself in charge of a program sinking under a $1.3 million deficit on an annual budget (for all programs) of about $3 million. Its teams were struggling internationally, and some of its most high-profile potential allies—Nash and former men's national team coach Jay Triano being two examples—had been alienated.

Desperate for a lifeline to keep the organization afloat, Parrish secured a meeting with executives at Maple Leaf Sports and Entertainment Ltd.—owners of the NBA's Toronto Raptors and the Air Canada Centre, along with the Toronto Maple Leafs.

"There was no case I could make, or that they would buy, that could convince them that we were a good place to spend their money," Parrish says. Just the same, he found a Santa Claus—albeit a cautious, pragmatic one—in MLSE, an organization popularly known as sporting Scrooges, and the tentative renewal of Canada Basketball began.

The deal was for about $350,000 over three years, and was the difference between Canada Basketball continuing to function and, well, no one knows what. "We did the deal just after I took over, and things were incredibly grim," Parrish says. "We didn't know if we could meet payroll or pay rent. Every day was day-to-day."

The money from MLSE kept the lights on, and belt-tightening slashed the deficit to about $800,000. Parrish helped organize a coalition to lobby the federal government specifically on behalf of team sports, an effort that paid off when $6 million in annual funding was secured, with Canada Basketball getting about $600,000. The support from MLSE and the clout provided by the likes of Raptors president Bryan Colangelo encouraged Nike to sign on for $250,000 over four years, and to provide gear for the teams.

With that added support, Canada Basketball showed that its teams could succeed on the floor. In 2009 Canada was one of just six countries to qualify for all four world championships. The under-17 men's team won bronze, just the fourth medal Canada has ever won at the world level.

To the well managed go the spoils: MLSE later approved a five-fold increase in its support for Canada Basketball in the form of a three-year agreement valued at about $1.5 million. But Parrish wasn't done. He had his sights set on a bigger prize: repatriating the greatest basketball player in the history of the country. It wouldn't be easy. (In 2013, MLSE re-upped for nearly $2 million over four years.)

Nash had retired from international competition after Canada failed to qualify for the 2004 Olympics. At the Tournament of the Americas the team had dropped a semi-final game to Puerto Rico, despite a performance from Nash that was good for the tournament MVP. Not long after, things fell apart.

Nash's close friend Jay Triano was fired. The organization claimed he was too expensive given that as an assistant coach with the Raptors he was only available to coach in the summer months. Nash railed against the decision in the press: "That's bullshit. [Triano's firing] is asinine. It's horrendous . . . I never say never, but I doubt if I'll ever play for Canada again.

"I think they fired a guy that is as big as anybody in Canada's basketball history. Canada's been to three Olympics in the last thirty years and he's been to all three [two as a player, one as a coach]. He's willing to coach our country. He's made sacrifices. Any talk to the contrary is bullshit. I think it was a really misguided decision and a shame.

"We had a good thing going. The only failure we had was [losing to] Puerto Rico last year. And for our team to make it to the semi-finals with the guys we took down? We should have never beat Brazil. We should have never almost beat Argentina in the early rounds. And we should have never beat Puerto Rico in the early rounds. And no offence to some of the guys on our team, but they had never played at that level before.

"For us to get to that level, Jay overachieved as a coach, we overachieved as a team. It pisses me off."

Nash signalled broadly that his days in a Canadian uniform were over: "I'm getting older. I have two children now. So I can't say never but it'd be pretty difficult, especially with a new coach and starting all over," he said. He never played for Canada again and largely kept his distance from the program for much of the next decade.

Leo Rautins took over as head coach in 2005, tasked with trying to lift a team without its best player and too soon to benefit from the explosion of Canadian talent that was inspired by Nash's exploits in the NBA. Canada failed to qualify for the 2006 World Championships or the 2008 Olympics. They squeaked into the 2010 Worlds only to finish twenty-second out of twenty-four teams. A once-competitive basketball country had only qualified for one Olympic tournament since 1988.

Looking ahead to London, Canada again failed to qualify for the Olympics. The influx of cash from MLSE and Nike was appreciated, but Parrish knew he needed Nash involved if he was going to successfully resuscitate the program in any sustainable way. The coming wave of Canadian players with NBA potential made timing an issue. By 2015 Olympic qualifying, Canada could have a starting five made completely of first-round NBA draft picks—something only the USA could match—and a roster so overflowing with NBA players that some won't make the final cut. But to get that talent in a Canadian uniform, the national team program would need to be relevant to those young players and there was no time to wait.

In the end Nash responded to overtures from Parrish but also from Barrett, his best friend in the national team program, who was living in Toronto and watching the wave of talent like a surfer on a beach seeing a massive wave build on the horizon. "When we played, we talked about doing something for the program when we're done playing," says Barrett, recalling how the seeds of their vision were planted on a dejected night out after they were eliminated from Olympic contention in 2003. "Steve is still playing, but if we waited it would be too late."

Nash's stature has already improved the program's finances.

In the past, the men's national team has operated on a budget of between $400,000 and $500,000 a season, while the top ten countries in the world tend to have budgets ranging from $1 to $2 million (some more than double that). Parrish is overseeing a booster group known as the "Sixth Man" that hopes to raise $4 million over the course of the 2016 Olympic cycle, and they're already halfway there. "It's amazing how powerful Steve getting on a conference call is . . . how galvanizing that is for these individuals," Parrish says.

"We've talked about this since we played for the national team, of how we could impact the program, how we could improve it, how we could hopefully leave it in a better place than when we got involved," Nash said when he was introduced in his new executive role. As if to suggest that Basketball Canada was emerging from the right end of a rags-to-riches story, Nash held court in a well-manicured press conference in the atrium of the Air Canada Centre, packed with media, a strong contingent from MLSE and former national team players. His hiring made news internationally and he marked the occasion by wearing a tailored grey suit with a black tie and red pocket square. "I guess it was a long time coming, but I didn't foresee it being this early."

The biggest challenge for Nash will be helping the national team mean as much to a new generation of players as it did to him and his peers. When Nash was trying to establish himself in Victoria, the national team—and to a lesser extent the B.C. provincial team—represented an essential portal to a wider world of basketball. To young players today, Ian Hyde-Lay sending grainy videotapes to U.S. college coaches sounds like something out of a quaint period piece. Between the end of Nash's international playing days and his appointment as general manager, top

Canadian prospects were more likely to have shown up on the radar of college and NBA scouts whether they were involved with the national team or not. With the rise of Amateur Athletic Union basketball in Canada, it became common for elite high school–age players to pass up national or provincial team training camps and tournaments that conflicted with major AAU events, which attract much more attention from U.S. college coaches. As someone who always dreamed of playing for Canada, Nash is now in the position of having to sell his dream to a group of players who won't necessarily share it.

Consider the differences between Nash's experiences and those of Andrew Wiggins, the Toronto-born prodigy projected as the Canadian hoopster most likely to approach some of Nash's achievements in the game. In 2009, when Wiggins was thirteen, a simple Google search led to a YouTube video entitled: "Andrew Wiggins, Best 13-year-old in the Nation?"—and the nation wasn't Canada, it was the United States. Nash hadn't even started playing serious basketball at age 13. By the time Wiggins was ready to declare for college, the clip of his barely teenaged self had been viewed a staggering 4.3 million times.

Wiggins left home in Thornhill, north of Toronto, to attend school in the U.S. as an eighth grader, which is just about the age Nash began to focus on basketball among all his sports and even then just so he could keep up with his friends. By his senior season at Huntington Prep in West Virginia, Wiggins had been at the top of various websites that track the progress of high school stars for three years, and been featured by the *Washington Post* and ESPN; he had attended the LeBron James Skills Academy and wowed the King himself with one baseline dunk—again captured on YouTube, complete with James's ecstatic reaction.

All of which is to say, in the post-Nash era, convincing great young players to play for their country is a different beast. It's much harder to make the program relevant to a generation of kids who get scouting reports compiled on them by websites like DraftExpress.com by the time they're in the tenth grade and spend their high school years trying to crack ESPN.com's prestigious top-100 prospect list. For Nash, playing for Canada was an essential outlet to the greater basketball universe and a key step in his climb to becoming a star in the NBA. For Nash as a general manager, the challenge is to make playing for their country an essential part of the basketball lives of the next generation, who have gained plenty of recognition independent from the national team experience.

"The national team doesn't have a monopoly anymore," Nash says, taking a welcome break from a grinding first season with the Los Angeles Lakers to talk about his passion project. "Kids have way too many options. For me, the national program is a phenomenal opportunity for these kids, but you have to build it out so that it really offers them a lot: whether they play on the national team or not they're supported, they're driven, they're coached, they're gaining experience and they're giving themselves, first and foremost, a chance to grow as players. And because of that the national team will grow and improve.

"And once we get them there, they'll want to be there because they can't miss it as far as their development, but also because all their countrymen and friends are on the team and they want to be there with them because they want to be part of that group. That's what we did, we just didn't have the resources."

Listening to Nash and his national team friends reflect on their years wearing the maple leaf on their chests is almost like listening to old pals talk about their best years in minor soccer or a high school run to the regional finals. It's refreshing and remarkably distinct from the big business of the NBA, where—as legendary coach Chuck Daly once accurately noted—you're not coaching a team, you're trying to find common ground among twelve corporations, each with their own agendas. Fortunately it's a job for which Nash is perfectly suited.

"The thing about Steve is even by the time he was in the NBA, he never lost his love for the game," says Todd MacCulloch, who played on the national team with Nash for three years and against him in the NBA for four seasons. "The 1999 Tournament of the Americas was one of the biggest tournaments I've ever played in, trying to qualify for the Olympics. We were staying in [a] nice place on the beach in San Juan [Puerto Rico] and we had a big win early in the tournament [against Argentina] and Nash says, 'Good job fellas, meet on the beach at six p.m. We're play-ing 500-up.' Everyone got in their trunks and Steve was throwing out a mini soccer ball he brought and we're run-ning around in the surf. It became a thing we did. He never lost focus on what was important.

"He was rooming with Andrew Mavis," says MacCulloch. "And they're heading back and forth one of those big exer-cise balls across the bed. The rules were it couldn't hit the floor or the ceiling. And you'd walk by their room for dinner and they'd be up to seventy-eight or something then they'd go back and they'd be up to ninety and then we'd have a film session. It was just like the Hanson Brothers in *Slap Shot* playing slot cars. He made his own fun and it was always fun being a teammate when he was the leader.

"But when it was time to play there was no more fierce competitor than Steve and no one who wanted to win more and who knew that you're not going to get it done on your own, that a team of five can beat one or two. His goal was to make people better."

If the national team was a family, Jay Triano was the father figure—though maybe the thoughtful, dutiful older brother is more accurate. Like Nash, Triano had been raised in the national team program. He grew up in the Niagara region, benefitting from the proximity of the U.S. border when it came to having his eyes opened to a higher level of competition. He played college basketball at Simon Fraser University—the Vancouver-based school that competed in the National Association of Intercollegiate Athletics (NAIA)—where he remains the school's all-time leading scorer and was good enough to be an eighth-round pick of the Los Angeles Lakers, though he never played in an NBA game. Triano was a central figure on the 1980s-era teams coached by Jack Donohue that were consistently among the top six in the world, a level the upcoming generation of Canadian teams, led by Nash and coached by Triano—the obvious hire for head coach when Nash and Barrett landed their executive roles—will aspire to reach or surpass.

The bond between Nash and Triano goes back nearly three decades: the coach shaped the character of the teams that Nash starred on and they reflect an ethic the pair hope to pass on to those that come into the program today.

Theirs is a basketball bromance, and Triano remembers the first time he laid eyes on his hoops crush like it was yesterday. Then a coach at SFU, he had made the ninety-minute crossing to the island so he could watch the national team train in Victoria and found himself at a summer league game at UVic.

Cue the soft lighting: "I saw this kid make this really great move and finish a layup with his left hand and I turned and asked someone: 'Who is the left-handed kid?'" says Triano. "And people were like, 'What left-handed kid?'

"It just turned out that even then Steve had a great left hand, so right away I put him down on my recruiting list."

Triano became Nash's most ardent suitor as he tried to recruit the point guard into his lineup at SFU. "Other guys would go to his basketball games, I remember going to his soccer games and standing beside his dad, John," says Triano, now an assistant coach with the Portland Trail Blazers in addition to his new national team duties. "I was recruiting him and wanted to show that I had interest in him as a person and show support for him overall, not just in basketball.

"When [St. Michael's University School] won the B.C. provincial championship, I got a photograph of him with the MVP trophy and the net around his neck blown up into a poster delivered to his house." It was a gesture that would be a clear violation of NCAA rules, but Triano paid no mind. "In the NAIA back then there were no illegal gifts and I was a pretty active recruiter."

It didn't work. Nash and Triano broke up—or at least broke off their engagement—on a stormy B.C. afternoon at the Tsawwassen Ferry Terminal, south of Vancouver. Nash had spent the day with Triano as the coach made a last-ditch effort to sell the point guard—by then a star on the B.C. basketball scene—on the merits of SFU. As Triano drove him to catch the boat to Vancouver Island and Nash's home in Victoria, the winds were high and when they arrived, they found out the ferry was delayed. Triano felt obligated to wait it out with his prospect, and as the minutes ticked on, they stopped talking as recruit and coach and began talking as friends. Nash had ambition. He wanted to see the world and conquer it through basketball. Leaving Victoria to play in Burnaby, B.C.— even for Triano—wasn't going to cut it.

"He didn't have a whole lot of offers, but Santa Clara was on to him and we had some time to kill and did some more chatting and he finally asked me about Santa Clara and said, 'If you were me, what would you do?'

"It was an easy call," says Triano. "You think about the kid first and you don't want them to have any regrets. You'd rather them aim high and if things don't work out you can always come back, and hopefully if you did a good job recruiting them they'll want to come play for you.

"So I told him he should go play in the NCAA and see what happened."

But Triano added a rejoinder: "Besides, I told him I would coach him anyway, because I said I was going to be head coach of the national team and he was going to be my best player."

Triano's willingness to sacrifice his own short-term self-interest for the sake of a prospective player forever remained a touchstone for Nash and arguably established a level of respect for the four years Triano coached the national team with Nash on it.

"He was great to coach because he was the hardest worker," says Triano. "Even though he came to the team as an NBA player he wanted to be treated like everyone else, he didn't want a first-class seat on the plane, he didn't want a single room on the road. He sat in the middle seat all the way to Sydney. He wanted to do things the right way; playing for the national team was a passion, it was special to him.

"I remember the first day of practice and the guys were on the bus waiting and everyone's like, 'Where's Steve?' and it turns out he's still in the gym getting up shots, and this is after we've just practiced for three hours. As a coach you don't have to say much when your best player is doing that. Guys start thinking, 'If he's still in the gym getting his three hundred threes up before he goes, maybe that's why he's in the NBA.' The next day there was no one on the bus, everyone stayed and got extra shots up. When you've got a leader like that, everyone feeds off of it and it makes it pretty easy to coach."

Nash carried the ball bags. He had a roommate. He sat in the middle seat in coach. And as a courtesy to the coaching staff, he never flashed his NBA card.

"We would be going over some screen-and-roll coverage and I'd lay it out and everyone would be nodding," says Triano. "And then after practice he'd pull me aside and say, 'You know, I'm way more comfortable if I can just play it this way.'

"And at that point in our careers he'd played against the screen-and-roll a lot more than I'd coached against it, so he knew what he was talking about, but he waited until he could pull me aside privately and raise it as a suggestion instead of second-guessing me in front of the team; it just shows a lot of respect and class."

But as much as playing for his country struck a deep patriotic chord for Nash, there was a pragmatic one that resonated as well. At that point in his NBA career, Nash was in desperate need of a team to call his own.

After a promising start to his NBA career, Nash went into a deep trough in his first year in Dallas in 1998–99. He was struggling with injuries that had yet to be properly diagnosed and was shooting a career-low 37.3 percent from the field on a bad Mavericks team; for the first and only time in his career, Nash was the subject of fans' scorn as they booed their new high-priced point guard for that most undeniable of reasons: he sucked.

That summer, the national team became something more than a place for Nash to reconnect with his friends and play for his flag. It became a refuge and a place where he could play basketball the way he played it growing up: freely and with friends. As the undisputed leader he could play with his mind clear and mend his fraying confidence.

"From a formative perspective, it was very vital for him to play early on," says Barrett. "You need three things to be [successful]. One, you need strong coaching. Second, you need talent. Third, you need the right training environment: you need the opportunity to make mistakes, you need to have the opportunity to have the ball in your hand and live and die with your decisions. Playing for the national team, Steve was able to get those types of experiences that he wasn't getting in the NBA earlier on, which actually helped him eventually in the NBA context.

"NBA people could see what he looked like with the ball in his hands against good competition. So in the end [the national team] helped him."

The national team had been at a bit of a low ebb, having finished a disappointing twelfth at the 1998 World Championships minus Nash thanks to the NBA lockout, with the effort costing head coach Steve Konchalski his job.

"For the young guys, it was 'Wait till we get to the next one, it's not going to be like this. When our group gets a chance to take over and do something, it's not going to be like this'," says Sherman Hamilton. "For the older guys, I think it was 'This is some bullshit.' And they knew their time was up."

In 1999, with Nash running the point and Triano on the bench, things turned around almost immediately.

"We got some much needed experience in those international climates where it's eat or be eaten, basically," says Hamilton. "And we needed that.

"We beat Argentina in that first game and from then on we just felt everyone else in our way, we're going to beat if we do the right things. We weren't cocky but we felt if we played the way we could play, we could beat anyone in that tournament, outside the U.S."

Nash's humility and brand of play were exactly what that team needed. And he was paid back in kind. Instead of doubts and boos, he had unquestioned support and a team willing to follow his lead.

"He brought us that confidence, but the group we had, we were all fighters, so it was perfect for Steve," says Hamilton. "Steve would try to will a bag of oranges to win a game, but he had a group of guys that were already seething and waiting to take that next step, so it was perfect timing.

"We lost to Puerto Rico [in the second round, 80–75] and we're in the locker room and that was one of those moments where you're pissed off and . . . you've got to take down the home country," says Hamilton. "That's a statement game and we lost it. And we're sitting there and we're pissed off and Steve came in and said, 'They can't beat us twice.' And sure enough they didn't." Nash and his teammates went on to beat Puerto Rico two days later in the semi-final, a game that had an Olympic berth on the line. Nash was the tournament MVP, as he scored twenty-six points and grabbed eight rebounds, while dishing out four assists in an 83–71 win.

Canada had qualified for their first Olympic tournament since 1988. For once, Canadian basketball was on the map. With the national media assembled to cover the Sydney Games, for a few weeks Nash and his teammates became Canada's Team. They finished first of six teams in their preliminary group, notching wins over powers like Spain and Yugoslavia, and losing only to Russia. It set up a seemingly favourable matchup for the playoff round as Canada drew France—fourth-place finishers in the other preliminary pool—in their quarter- final game. A win there and Canada would be playing for its first Olympic medal in basketball since 1936. But the magical run ended abruptly when a pair of French guards took turns forcing the ball out of Nash's hands, pushing the already physical brand of international basketball to the limit. Canada lost 68–63, ending their tournament and leaving Nash in tears.

But getting to the Olympics had provided a clear signal that Nash's best basketball was ahead of him and his ceiling was higher than anyone may have thought. It was a prelude to his breakout 2000–01 season, in which he leveraged his virtuoso Olympic experience into career highs in every offensive category and a playoff berth for the Mavericks, and it started in Roberto Clemente Coliseum in stifling San Juan, Puerto Rico, in front of a rabid crowd of twelve thousand in full throat.

All of them wanted the same thing: to see Canada go down. On the line was the last spot in the 2000 Games, on the floor was the best Puerto Rico could offer, a team with a handful of NBA players and some hardened pros who had played in the island's domestic professional league and in Europe.

"It was for all the marbles in international play. We were in a situation where we could really show the world we were ready to compete. That game in Puerto Rico, with twelve or thirteen thousand people there, all of them against us, that was one of the biggest games I've ever been in and no one thought we could win it, except us," says Hamilton, who hit seven free throws in the final three minutes to help seal the win. "And we went in there and did and Steve had a lot to do with it. He played one of the best games I've seen him play.

"I remember one time they were getting into Steve— and international ball, you tug and grab and all that stuff— and Steve got by, rose up, hit a jumper, got fouled and just held his follow-through [after the whistle]. It was just one of those 'No matter what you do to me, I'm going to do what I do.'"

Ideally there should have been many more moments like that for Canada in international basketball. In his new executive role, Nash has a chance and the tools to rectify that by doing what he's always done with a ball in his hands: galvanizing the group; finding a way to make the whole as strong as possible and the experience itself resonate with the best instincts of the individuals involved.

It might be his toughest play yet.

"One of the main pillars of the program is for guys to have successful individual careers. I really want to give them that opportunity to help them realize their dreams and goals and play a long time and make a lot of money and have a big impact on the kids that come after them," Nash says.

"But as a by-product of that, we'll have a great national team, and as a perk for them I want them to experience what I've experienced playing for the national team: have a great time, playing with my friends—those guys are going to be my friends for the rest of my life. I'm as close to the guys on the national team as I am with my friends from high school or college. That is a perk and I want them to experience it."

What Nash wants and what he believes in, he can often will to happen. Nash thinks teams are important. He believes it and he believes in Canada. And as we've seen with the kid from Victoria, his belief is a powerful, powerful thing.

CHAPTER FiVE

Rising in Phoenix:
The MVP Years

Standing at a podium in Phoenix on a spring afternoon in 2005, Steve Nash looked out on his basketball life. He'd just been presented with the Maurice Podoloff Trophy, his reward for being voted the most valuable player in the undisputed top league of the second most popular sport on the planet.

On a global game's biggest stage, he'd been deemed the most important performer. The familiar faces in the crowd were many and welcome. His parents, John and Jean Nash, had made the trip, as had his sister, Joann. Jay Triano, Nash's beloved former coach with the national team, had flown out to see the ceremony, calling it one of the great moments in the history of Canadian sport.

"A once-in-a-lifetime thing," John Nash called it. As difficult as it was to fathom that his son was being recognized as a sport's premier practitioner, it was even harder to believe that, a year later, Steve Nash—he of just a single

Division I scholarship offer and that boo-worthy season in Dallas—would become just the ninth player in history to win back-to-back MVP trophies. One MVP was improbable enough, of course. Not only did he become the first Canadian to win the award, he became only the second non-American to win it (although Hakeem Olajuwon, Nigerian by birth, competed for the U.S. during the 1996 Olympic Games in Atlanta) and, after Magic Johnson, Bob Cousy and Oscar Robertson, only the fourth point guard (fifth, if you include Allen Iverson). Given his underdog's lot, perhaps it surprised no one to learn that Nash, as the fifteenth overall pick in 1996, was also the lowest drafted player to be named MVP and the only back-to-back MVP listed under 6-foot-6.

"I guess it's an incredible oddity in many ways," Nash said. "My neighbourhood didn't have any NBA players . . . and obviously hockey is the first, second and third story in our country. To be here is very unlikely. And at the same time, I think that makes it a great accomplishment for me to cherish, in that there [were] a lot of obstacles just to be a professional basketball player."

On that first crowning, it was only fitting that Nash invited his Phoenix Suns teammates to the lectern to accept the trophy along with him. Winners of twenty-nine games the campaign before, the Suns had been the surprise story of that NBA season. The arrival of Nash as a free agent had proven the missing ingredient to turn coach Mike D'Antoni's convention-defying offence into the league's most formidable point-producing engine.

They'd led the league in scoring while averaging more than 110 points a game; the season before, NBA teams had put up 93.4 points each on a typical night. They'd led the league in wins with a remarkable sixty-two, then the third-biggest year-over-year turnaround in the NBA record books. They'd spurred talk of a much-celebrated revival of the kind of free-flowing, entertaining style that had ruled during the league's 1980s boom but had fallen out of favour in the increasingly hyper-coached, defence-obsessed NBA of the 1990s and beyond.

Certainly, the entire roster deserved its share of credit: Amar'e Stoudemire was a former Rookie of the Year Award winner whose high-scoring season had proven him to be one of the most explosive big men in the game; Shawn Marion, acquired with the draft pick that sent Nash to Dallas all those years ago, had been an All-Star before Nash arrived. But it was difficult to argue with the idea that Nash was the linchpin of the operation. Nash led the league in assists, led all guards in field-goal percentage, ranked sixth in the league in three-point shooting accuracy. The MVP vote would be close; Shaquille O'Neal of the Miami Heat would get fifty-eight first-place votes to Nash's sixty-five from the panel of media members charged with the decision. The 7-foot-1 O'Neal's arrival had transformed Miami from near-.500 mediocrity to title contention, to be sure. But Nash's presence, in many eyes, had done something more special. Along with instantaneously turning a bad team into a good one, it had turned Phoenix into a sort of roundball Utopia. It was a place where plenty of the NBA product's undesirable qualities appeared to have been banished in favour of a more joyous expression of the game. In Phoenix's run-and-fun system, there was no room for the slow-it-down, football-style play calling that had taken over parts of the NBA. There was no place for one-on-five ball-hogging or incessant over-dribbling. Instead, there was a new appetite for the building blocks of the childhood game—the running, passing and uninhibited shooting that introduced so many young players to the joy of the sport in the first place.

Upon joining the Suns during Nash's first MVP season, journeyman forward Paul Shirley said he was struck by the positivity that seemed to imbue the franchise at every level. Coming from a grim stint as a pro in Russia—a situation Shirley described as "mega mercenary"—he had counted himself "ready to be done with basketball." But just as the Suns breathed welcome life into the league, they renewed Shirley's faith in sport's transformational powers.

"It starts at the top. They had a really great organization. Everything was run well. It's interesting how good seems to attract good," Shirley said. "Everyone in that culture, from the secretary to the assistant trainer, was generally a positive human being and then they were able to get a star who was also this same sort of personality and that, as it turns out it, was significantly more important than people realize. At one point I had a tryout with San Antonio and got a chance to talk with [Spurs GM] R.C. Buford . . . What [Buford] had learned was if you can get your best player to also be your best guy then everything else kind of lines up. If that dominant player's personality takes control of the locker room, everything is going to be all right. And that was the case of Steve in Phoenix."

From the inside, and from the outside, Nash's influence was more than obvious.

"He's the glue," Frank Hamblen, coach of the L.A.

Stephen Nash

Stephen came to Smu just after school started in grade 11, making headlines everywhere. This star basketball player is also a stud off the courts gaining attention form many female admirers. Steve has many friends across town and has shared his heart with a "few" ladies. Although these ladies would have loved to be his, he only has room in his heart for a very special lady from Belmont. Contrary to what Steve says he is a stud and will be one forever. Steve's first year of Rugby landed him a spot on the infamous 1st XV for 3 games. Steve will have opportunities next year that will enable him to expand his athletic horizons and will likely be seen in the NBA one day.

As a teenager in Victoria, B.C., Steve Nash benefits from an unexpected confluence of athletic talent, great coaching and opportunities to compete.

Eli Pasquale puts together one of the best careers in Canadian university sports, and gives a teenaged Nash crucial advice: "If you want to play in the NBA, you should decide right now."

Coach Ken Shields follows Pasquale from Sudbury to Victoria, where he too is impressed by the talent and focus of a young Nash.

Directing traffic for the Santa Clara University Broncos.

In 1996, Nash joins the Phoenix Suns behind guards Jason Kidd and Kevin Johnson, watching and playing when he can.

After a difficult first season in Dallas, Nash gets his mojo back playing for Team Canada at the 1999 Tournament of the Americas, taking on Jason Kidd and the U.S. squad.

Nash flashes his national team's placement in their pool after upsetting Yugoslavia at the 2000 Olympics in Sydney, Australia.

In January 2002, Nash and Dallas teammate Michael Finley congratulate coach Don Nelson on his 1000th career win.

"To compare Steve Nash with John Stockton borders on the absurd," says Gonzaga coach Dan Fitzgerald in 1995. That would change. Here, Nash and Stockton go head-to-head in the 2002 playoffs.

He can jump. In the 2003 playoffs, Nash puts a signature layup around towering San Antonio Spur Tim Duncan.

Back in Phoenix, Nash and
Amar'e Stoudamire propel one
of the most dynamic offenses
the NBA had seen in decades.

Nash and Stoudamire combine
for the pick-and-roll that just
keeps giving.

Nash goes to the basket in
2008 with Kobe Bryant
looking on. It's hard to
imagine the two leaders ever
becoming teammates.

Nash is awarded his second
MVP title, in 2006, prior to a
home game against the Clippers.

Nowitzki tries in vain to stop his
friend's drive, a move the 2007 MVP
enjoyed watching more when he and
Nash wore the same uniform.

Only in the NBA could a six-foot-three guy look so small—lining up during
2010 All-Star festivities between long-time Dallas teammate and close friend
Dirk Nowitzki and the Spurs' Tim Duncan.

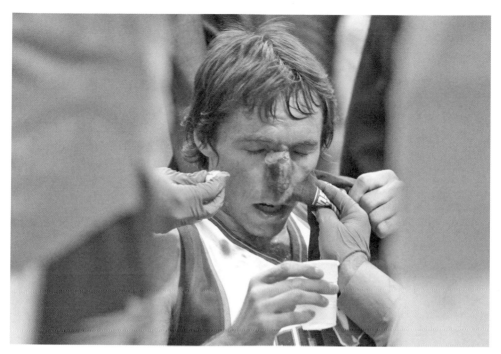

Looking more like the rugby or hockey player he could have been, Nash shakes off a bloodied nose, courtesy of a collision that floored Spurs guard Tony Parker in the 2007 playoffs, and a ripped brow in the conference semifinals in 2010, with Parker showing a little respect for his rival's toughing it out.

These guys love to play against each other: Parker and Nash get it on at Nash's 2011 Showdown in Chinatown fundraiser in New York City. That's retired New York Red Bulls captain Claudio Reyna in the foreground.

Nash always had a different style for an NBA star, but the velvet is pushing it. He receives an honorary Doctor of Laws at the University of Victoria, a school that taught him lots about the game that made him a superstar, even though he was never a student there.

Can this possibly work? In 2012, Nash joins Dwight Howard and Kobe Bryant on a star-studded L.A. Lakers team that would get swept by eventual finalists San Antonio in the first round of the playoffs.

Lakers, had acknowledged that season, speaking for much of the basketball-watching world. "He's the guy that pulled it all together for them."

That Nash wasn't enjoying a career-defining moment as a member of the Dallas Mavericks—that he was being honoured for his work in the first season of his second go-round with the Suns—spoke to an undeniable truth about his improbable run. Just as the Victoria-based doubters had pooh-poohed his chances as a collegian; just as skeptics in Phoenix and Dallas had called into question his value when he was selected with a first-round draft pick and was later traded for one, the doubts never really ceased. In his six seasons with Dallas, it hadn't seemed to matter that Nash had established himself as a perennial All-Star. It hadn't seemed to matter that he'd been instrumental in Dirk Nowitzki's development, made big shots in playoff wins, proved to be tireless in his work ethic. He was still Steve Nash; in the eyes of others, his success was anything but guaranteed.

In the summer of 2004, Nash's contract with the Mavericks came to an end and the point guard became an unrestricted free agent, free to accept offers from all thirty of the NBA's teams. Dallas owner Mark Cuban expressed his uncertainty about Nash's long-term viability as an NBA player in the plainest terms possible—he put a price on it. Nash, after all, had turned 30 in February, and Cuban had more than a few well-considered reasons for feeling iffy about making a long-term commitment worth multi-millions to a point guard of that age. Cuban, an enthusiastic supporter of basketball's burgeoning embrace of statistical analysis, knew well that the historic performance arc of players past their 30th birthday didn't offer promising returns on a big-dollar investment. John Hollinger, the analytics pioneer whom Cuban had once called his favourite basketball writer and who would later be hired as a senior executive with the Memphis Grizzlies, had written convincingly about the perils of employing players—especially point guards—whose ages began with the number three. Cuban would say later that Dallas support staff familiar with Nash's injury and medical history advised him that the NBA grind would prove untenable to Nash's fragile frame sooner rather than later.

"All the advice I got from everybody we had was that he was going to fall apart," Cuban would reflect years later. "He proved us wrong—and more power to him. I give him a lot of credit. He proved me definitely wrong . . . The thing about Steve is his discipline. I knew he was disciplined, but I thought he would fall apart before it mattered." If there was a single issue that gave Cuban cause for concern it was spondylolisthesis, a congenital condition that caused Nash's vertebra to slip and trigger a nerve that tightened his hamstring. The feeling was that managing the condition would eventually prove too much and Nash's ability to play at a high level would be compromised.

Unknown to Cuban was that his doubts would only drive Nash to try even harder—it is the Steve Nash way. In July, after the Suns shipped a twelve-person recruiting team to Dallas on a private jet to offer Nash a five-year contract worth more than $60 million, Cuban balked at the opportunity to match Phoenix's price. Dallas's initial offer to Nash had run only four years and didn't approach $12 million a season. Phoenix's willingness to tack on an extra year—and more than a few extra millions—spoke volumes to the free agent.

"I'm a little surprised," Nash said then, "that [the Mavericks] didn't value me a little more."

The truth is the Mavericks were a house divided. Coach and GM Don Nelson was a vehement proponent of paying whatever it took to keep Nash. Insiders have marked the moment Nash left Dallas as the beginning of the end of Nelson's relationship with Cuban (he would resign from the operation a little less than two seasons later). Certainly Nelson didn't hide his displeasure with the situation in his public comments after Nash left.

"We've lost a big part of our team and are getting nothing in return. I never dreamed we'd lose Steve Nash. We're not going to be as good without Steve, that's for sure," Nelson said.

Said Cuban at the time: "Short term, Steve will be difficult to replace. Long term, it was best for the organization. We just weren't comfortable facing the prospect of having little or no flexibility and the core of our team being thirty-five or older." In essence, he called Nash's bluff: would the ultimate team player leave a perennial championship contender where he could continue starring alongside his best friend in basketball? Was the Suns money enough to convince Nash that it was time to become a franchise player? After a career spent first as a back-up singer and then the team-sports version of playing rhythm guitar, Nash was about to take centre stage.

On paper, Nash was joining a bad team. And Nash the athlete had almost never taken a backward step, the injury-exacerbated difficulties of that first Dallas season notwithstanding. Progress was essential to his entire basketball being—start at the bottom and climb ever upward, rung by rung. But now Nash was leaving one of the best teams in the NBA to return to the Phoenix Suns, a proud franchise to be sure, but one coming off a 29–53 season, their second-worst mark since their expansion-year inauguration in 1968–69. It would be counter to Nash's reputation to suggest that he made the move from Dallas for the money, but it's hard not to conclude that he was doing exactly that, given he was leaving an NBA title contender—the Mavericks having finished their fourth straight season of fifty or more wins—for a team that missed the playoffs by fourteen games.

But there are different kinds of losing seasons. In the NBA, selective losing can have a real purpose. Just as in battle there are times when a strategic retreat is in order, NBA teams occasionally take a step back in order to make a great leap forward. On January 5, 2004, the Phoenix Suns made just such a move, and it is without argument that one of the greatest shows in the NBA would never have happened without it. On that cold winter afternoon Phoenix GM Bryan Colangelo's flight out of Toronto was delayed after a Suns loss to the Raptors. It left him just enough time to connect with New York Knicks president and general manager Isiah Thomas to make a deal that rocked the NBA and changed Canadian basketball. It was a seven-player trade, but there was really only one name that caught widespread attention: the Suns, after all, were sending their top player of the moment, point guard Stephon Marbury, back to his Big Apple stomping grounds. It was easy to understand why the Knicks wanted the trade.

Marbury was not just a great point guard, he was a great New York point guard—born and raised on Coney Island, he had built his body on training runs up and down the stairwells of the infamous public housing towers in which he grew up. He had made his name winning city championships at Abraham Lincoln High School in Brooklyn. He was, in some ways, made for the Madison Square Garden marquee, complete with a self-styled nickname: Starbury.

And what of the Suns? The logic seemed less obvious. Why, in a talent-driven league, would you cash in your team's leading scorer, a two-time All-Star, for a package that included Howard Eisley, Maciej Lampe, Antonio McDyess, Charlie Ward, Milos Vujanic, and a couple of first-round picks?

"With this deal, it appears Phoenix is throwing in the towel on this season," respected former coach and analyst Jack Ramsay said. "Can the Suns do something profitable with the two first-round draft picks from the Knicks? Only time will tell."

Indeed, there was a long game in place, and ever so slowly the chess pieces were being moved so that Colangelo and the Suns could get their man: a shaggy-haired point guard then playing for the Dallas Mavericks.

"This is a big picture kind of move, and a bold move," Colangelo said. "We didn't have flexibility under the cap, and we were hamstrung by some contracts. This allows us to be a player in free agency if we choose to. This is not a talent-for-talent deal."

The Suns' deal cost them their best player, but it also allowed them to shed some heavy salaries that would have prevented them from participating in the free agent market the following summer and could have resulted in a $20 or $25 million luxury tax bill. All of that for what? Even with Marbury averaging 18 points and 7.1 assists per game, the Suns had gotten off to a 4–18 start and were almost certain to miss the playoffs a year after being bounced in the first round.

"We looked at our situation and said, 'Do we want to be five, six or seven [in the Western Conference], or do we want to be one, two or three?'" said Bryan Colangelo. "Well, we want to be one, two or three. So our best shot to get up there was to make this deal because now we have options to improve. The timing was right for us."

For Colangelo the move was about trying to finish a family basketball legacy that stretched back decades. What was a lost half season? His father, Jerry, was already a giant in the sport. The scion of Italian immigrants who grew up in working-class Chicago Heights, the elder Colangelo was the star of his own Horatio Alger myth as rich as anything that ever hit the printed page. He would reminisce about keeping a salt shaker in his pocket when he left the house hungry should he happen to swipe a shopkeeper's tomato. Growing up, he made himself through sports, starring in baseball and playing basketball at the University of Illinois. Colangelo was selling tuxedos when he reached out to a client and was able to land a job with the expansion Chicago Bulls.

After some early success with the Bulls he was given the job of general manager with the expansion Phoenix Suns at age 28, making him the youngest to hold the position in the NBA. He arrived in the desert on March 1, 1968, with a wife, three young children, and $200 in his wallet. It was raining hard that day, as the story goes. Years later Jerry Colangelo said he remembered smelling the orange blossoms in the air and believing that, even though he was far from home and working without a safety net of any kind, everything was going to be all right.

It was. The Suns became a model expansion franchise despite losing the infamous coin toss that determined who would pick first in the 1969 draft. In the league's offices in New York Colangelo called "heads" and the Kennedy 50-cent piece came up tails. The Milwaukee Bucks got the pick and took Kareem Abdul-Jabbar (then Lew Alcindor), the centre of six NBA championship teams who, nearly a quarter of a century since he last played, is still the NBA's all-time leading scorer. Colangelo's Suns thrived regardless, even if the second pick that year turned out to be a journeyman centre named Neal Walk. The Suns made the NBA Finals in 1976; in 1987, in the midst of scandal that saw three players indicted on charges of possessing and trafficking in marijuana and cocaine, Colangelo put together a group to buy the team that had employed him for nearly twenty years.

They finished 28–54 that season but set an NBA record with a 27-win turnaround in 1988–89 and advanced to the Western Conference final to start a run of thirteen straight post-season appearances. Missing from the franchise's CV, however, was a championship.

By the time the Suns made their next appearance in the NBA Finals they were one of the leading franchises in all of sports. They opened American West Arena in time for the 1992–93 season and won a franchise record sixty-two games during Charles Barkley's first season with the team.

They lost the Finals to Michael Jordan and the Chicago Bulls in six games, but that was about the only thing that went wrong—after all, everyone in the NBA lost to Jordan. The Suns had become the top revenue-earning team in the NBA, despite Phoenix being the seventeenth largest market in the United States. Jerry Colangelo's team didn't make money by accident: they were one of the first teams to generate arena revenue with naming rights and premium seat licensing.

The team's success, in turn, was changing the face of the city. When the franchise started they were the first professional sports franchise in the market and remained that way for twenty years. Colangelo's vision, ambition and the Suns' example, however, set big plans into play. In 1999 the *Arizona Republic* named Colangelo the state's sporting figure of the half century, an easy call considering he was the one man directly involved in bringing Arizona not only its pro basketball team, but hockey's Phoenix Coyotes in 1996 and baseball's Diamondbacks in 1998. "If this had been a horse race, Colangelo would have been Secretariat," the paper declared.

"It's amazing how far we've come," Jerry Colangelo said. "To see the transformation, to see the city become what it has as you fast-forward the clock, it's pretty phenomenal. In 1968, there was very little history here. And now look. We're one of just a handful of cities with four major league franchises. We've got a strong Arizona State program. The Phoenix Open. NASCAR. The Super Bowl. The Fiesta Bowl. The NBA All-Star Game twice during that period. Major League Baseball. All the venues that have been built.

"It's really been kind of an amazing, frantic period of

time. And really, much of it has taken place in the last ten, twelve years. I feel grateful that I was brought here when I was, and was given an opportunity to help make some things happen. But there was no game plan."

But when it came to having the Suns emerge again as contenders for an NBA championship; when it came to a son helping a father capture the one thing he'd never been able to claim for himself, there very much was a game plan, and Nash was very much at the centre of it. While Cuban calculated the risk of paying Nash and deemed it outsized, the Suns were happy to count themselves all in, acknowledging they were taking a risk on a risk-taking point guard.

"I disagreed [with Cuban's assessment]," is how Jerry Colangelo explains his thinking in retrospect. "I believed that he was not going to break down, that that was not going to be the case. And even if he had an extra year on the contract and it might come back to bite us, we were willing to do that. It was a non-issue. People talk about the times you miss in this business. But there are times you hit pay dirt. And Steve Nash is one of the most popular players ever to wear the Suns jersey."

Nash's popularity upon his return to Phoenix owed its rise to a confluence of characters. Bryan and Jerry Colangelo were looking to remake a franchise. Nash was bent on justifying the bulging contract he'd earned. And Mike D'Antoni was making his latest attempt at establishing himself as an NBA head coach with staying power.

The West Virginia–bred son of a high-school basketball-coach father and a Democratic activist mother, D'Antoni's pro basketball ambitions never really came to fruition on this side of the Atlantic. After a notable career as a collegian at Marshall University, he'd played about 130 games, mostly as a backup, for the NBA's Kansas City Kings (he finished his NBA run averaging 3.3 points a game). He also played fifty games for the Spirits of St. Louis in the now-defunct American Basketball Association. But he found his athletic calling in Europe, where he starred for more than a decade with Simac Milan, an Italian-league powerhouse (one that would adopt a number of other sponsor names in D'Antoni's time with the club). It wasn't the NBA, but it was more than a good life. D'Antoni made a six-figure salary, drove a team-provided Maserati and lived in a gratis flat. And he was hardly an anonymous figure. In Italy, sellout crowds were rabid and engaged, and D'Antoni was enough of a star that a rare American who grew up watching him—a future NBA prospect named Kobe Bryant—adopted D'Antoni's No. 8 as his own when he first broke into the NBA. (Kobe's father, Joe, was another NBA castoff who made a career on Italy's hardwood, where a school-aged Kobe would occasionally entertain the crowd with halftime shooting exhibitions). By the day of his retirement as a player in 1990, D'Antoni had led his team to five Italian league titles and a couple of Euroleague championships, and he'd been named the greatest point guard in the history of the Italian game. But D'Antoni knew that adoration, in Italy, was hardly unconditional.

"You play one bad game and they are on you," D'Antoni once said of Italy's basketball fans. "My third year here I missed a last-second shot, and the next day's headline was, 'D'Antoni Is a Traitor to Simac.'"

The requisite thick skin he'd developed as a star player in Europe served him well when he segued into coaching. On the bench, he made his bones in Italy, too, winning multiple titles in Milan. But the NBA remained a dream, and he took more than a few swings at finding success there. He worked as the Denver Nuggets' director of player personnel in 1997–98, was promoted to head coach during the lockout shortened 1998–99 campaign, and was promptly fired when the Nuggets won just fourteen games. He worked as a scout for the San Antonio Spurs and an assistant coach for the Portland Trail Blazers before he found his way back to Italy for a successful season at Benetton Treviso, where he worked under legendary European general manager Maurizio Gherardini.

Gherardini lauded D'Antoni for his infectious optimism: "Mike always said, 'There are no problems, only solutions.'" And perhaps that helps explain why, after that season in Treviso, he took a job as an assistant coach in Phoenix, where the Suns had finished ten games below .500. Perhaps it explains why, when head coach Frank Johnson was fired after an 8–13 beginning to the 2003–04 season, D'Antoni agreed to become Johnson's successor.

"It wasn't my intention to be a head coach right away," D'Antoni said at the time. "I was happy as hell being an assistant, especially with this group we have. But always in the back of your mind, if the opportunity presented itself— anywhere—I would have jumped on it. This is the . . . thing that I want to be successful at."

D'Antoni was once dubbed "the world's greatest contrarian" by an anonymous associate, quoted in the *New York Times*. And soon enough the NBA would understand why. The conventional wisdom in the NBA's tightly knit coaching fraternity had long been established: run-and-gun teams that emphasize offence over defence, teams that don't employ a dominant player in the post—these were teams that would not succeed. D'Antoni, billed as a run-and-gun offensive guru, was neither a part of the NBA coaches' old boy network, nor did he appear to aspire to be a part of it.

"We are going to try to be exciting," D'Antoni vowed upon taking over from Johnson. "We are going to try to put up a lot of points. We have the talent, physical capabilities—a nice style of basketball that's fun for the players."

The contrarian in D'Antoni saw possibilities in the Suns that few others might have. Stoudemire was a power forward not a centre, but D'Antoni played him there. Marion was a small forward not a power forward, but he manned that post for Suns teams. It was an alignment that is almost conventional now—the Miami Heat won an NBA championship in 2011–12 "playing small," with power forward Chris Bosh at centre and frequent small forward LeBron James often at power forward—but at the time it seemed like a gimmick and one unlikely to work, based on the previous 50 years of NBA history.

More traditional NBA approaches relied upon a seven-footer at centre with the ability to pound the opposition with high-percentage shots close to the basket. The likes of Stoudemire and Bosh were just as comfortable, sometimes more comfortable, making their contributions in different ways, often initiating the offence far from the basket with a pick-and-roll play. So many sequences in D'Antoni's vision of the Suns offence began with Stoudemire setting a pick on Nash's defender—essentially standing in the defender's way to offer Nash a beat of free space. Nash's options, then, were endless. If the defenders switched—that is, if the man guarding Stoudemire immediately began to guard Nash and vice versa—Stoudemire could usually exploit his advantage in size and strength on a smaller man, or Nash could exploit his edge in quickness on a larger foe. If the defence didn't react quickly enough, a timely Nash jump shot could fly. Or Stoudemire could find himself open for a jump shot, or an easy slash to the hoop. As a bread-and-butter play, it would prove incredibly effective, even if more traditional tacticians would have shuddered at the idea of an offence's biggest body spending so much time so far from the basket.

"I don't want to go with conventional thinking," D'Antoni would say during his Phoenix tenure. "I don't care if it's always been done this way. Now, that might be the right way to do it. But that's not the reason to do it."

D'Antoni struggled in his early throes as Phoenix's head coach; the team went 21–40 under his watch for the remainder of 2003–04. But Nash's arrival in the summer of 2004 changed everything. They were, as coach and point guard, an ideal match.

"I think two things collided to make it a great combination," said Dan D'Antoni, Mike's older brother and a Phoenix assistant coach. "One, you had a guy with skills, a very smart player in Steve who reads the floor with the ball and was exceptional in the pick-and-roll. Along comes Mike, who opens the floor up for him. The pick-and-roll, the basic thing we did in Phoenix, obviously fits right into

Steve's talents. From there, that fit, we had a great finisher in Amar'e. We had [three-point shooters] to keep the defence honest shooting from the wings. Add all that up—that allowed Steve to be Steve."

There was one other element that D'Antoni's Suns would be based on and it was speed. He wanted the game played at a pace that few other teams could withstand physically and which only the Suns could properly execute. Their mantra became "seven seconds or less"—the thinking being that the best scoring opportunities come before the twenty-four-second clock ticked below seventeen. First choice was a layup on the run; second choice was a wide-open three-pointer in transition. If either of those options were unavailable, the preferred course was to get the ball to Nash, spread the floor and let him turn the defence inside out with a dizzying array of pick-and-rolls. It was essentially a constant fast break and it put the rest of the NBA on its collective heels.

"Playing the Suns is like being a passenger in a car going seventy-five miles an hour," then New Jersey Nets coach Lawrence Frank said in Jack McCallum's book on the 2005–06 Suns, aptly titled *Seven Seconds or Less*. "When you're driving, like they are, you feel comfortable. But when you're the passenger, you're uncomfortable. The trick is how to figure out to be a driver. But they don't let you do that."

The strategy made the Suns heretics in some ways. For years the game had slowed and calcified, in part as a response to teams trying to solve elite talents like Michael Jordan. Good coaching and solid fundamentals were equated to slow, controlled play that often ended with a single player in isolation going against a set defence late in the shot clock.

Jordan, the Chicago Bulls legend, was in ascendance in the late 1980s, earning his first league MVP award in 1987–88. But when he led the Bulls against the Detroit Pistons in the Eastern Conference finals for the first time, Pistons coach Chuck Daly was determined to put him on the floor, as Motown's "Bad Boys" implemented the "Jordan Rules," a defensive strategy that called for double-teaming Jordan and fouling him hard whenever he drove to the basket. By the time Jordan and the Bulls were at their peak in the mid-1990s, the approach had spread like a virus throughout the NBA, with Pat Riley and the New York Knicks taking the tactic to the extreme, turning clutch-and-grab defence into a science.

As a result scoring was plummeting across the NBA; from a high in the three-point-line era (beginning 1979–80) of 110.8 during the 1984–85 season, the league average bottomed out at a quicksand-like 93.4 in 2003–04. It was the lowest average for a full NBA season since 1954–55, the year the league introduced the shot clock in order to speed up the game and increase scoring.

The Suns' innovations couldn't have come a moment too soon. In a few short years, many of the team's principles would be proven statistically sound. But at the time, the simple math of the three-point shot—which made sinking 33-out-of-100 from beyond the arc as effective as shooting 50 percent from inside it—hadn't been so widely embraced. When the Suns launched 2026 three-pointers in 2004–05 it was a whopping 734 more—or nearly nine more per game—than the league average. But the Suns weren't just shooting more from the field, they were converting those shots at a league-best 39.3 percent, compared to the league average of 35.6 percent. The league began to catch on and the average number of attempted threes has increased every year since Phoenix broke the mould in 2004–05. Similarly, D'Antoni's logic for getting shots off quickly, before the defence could get set, seems like common sense now; but, at the time, the league reacted to both strategies like he'd just told everyone that chocolate milkshakes were a new health food—it would be nice, but get real.

By the end of Nash and D'Antoni's first year together in Phoenix, the numbers supported the Suns' uptempo approach. The open floor and the increased pace meshed perfectly with his point guard's rare ability to play efficiently at full speed, and the team led the NBA in scoring with 110.4 points a game. No NBA team had cracked that mark in the previous ten years.

At the helm, Nash was the perfect player in the perfect system. Nash could be Nash in part because of the way D'Antoni's schemes opened up the floor for a creative point guard to penetrate. More conventional approaches varied, of course, but they generally hinged on the presence of two big men in or around the painted area.

"Mike was really the first one that came into the NBA and put the four players outside and only one guy in the lane," Dan D'Antoni said.

This allowed Nash more room to manoeuvre. With just one big-framed teammate stationed down low, it usually meant a penetrating Nash only had to worry about one big-framed defender providing resistance on his sorties to the rim.

"It changed the whole game. It changed the whole NBA," Dan D'Antoni said. "I mean, Miami won [the NBA championship in 2012] doing our stuff. That's how they did it, just opening the floor up." It was hardwood heaven, and Nash was basketball St. Peter.

Perhaps the groundwork for success was laid before the Nash-era Suns ever ran a fast break or bombed a three-pointer or flushed an alley-oop. By pairing D'Antoni and Nash with a cast that included Stoudemire and Marion, future All-Star Joe Johnson, and veteran regulars Quentin Richardson and Leandro Barbosa, maybe the Suns were destined to shine a light on the beauty of ball-zipping, free-flowing basketball that would make the Dallas Mavericks, once thought to be at the vanguard of streetball-under-the-NBA-spotlight, look positively conservative.

Nash, in the off-season before he would become the player nobody thought he could be, embraced the job of being as physically prepared as he could be. He took on two-a-day workouts with Rick Celebrini, a Vancouver-based physiotherapist with whom he had worked earlier in his playing days. Their sessions were a pre-emptive attack on the mileage-related injuries that tend to beset athletes of a certain age. Nash had long put a priority on such training on account of the spondylolisthesis, which predisposed his hamstrings and back to stiffening up (and is the reason he usually spent his time "on the bench" actually lying supine on the sideline next to it, with towels or a ball propping up his head as he watched the action). But Nash, perhaps in part because he was fully aware of the bet being made against his durability in Dallas, devoted unprecedented energy to this particular round of off-season tuning. Indeed, the way Celebrini told it, Nash underwent a biomechanical overhaul of sorts.

"We changed the way he ran and especially the way he changed direction," Celebrini said at the time. "We both recognized that there were ways in which he moved that were a direct result of his weaknesses and past injuries. We had to break down those movements and slowly re-create them through repetition. By correcting movement dysfunctions, we are able to prevent injury, optimize the biomechanical efficiency of the body and bring about performance enhancement."

Said Nash of Celebrini's regimens: "They allow me to prevent injury, sustain fitness and maintain my level of play through all of these games despite having a bad back."

Celebrini, as much as he's been a key member of Nash's support team, has long declined credit for Nash's success: "Steve is Steve because Steve has made Steve."

In the ensuing years Nash would become known for flying Celebrini to his NBA destination of the moment to have Celebrini observe his movement patterns and look for imbalances in need of correction.

"He'll go down on the court with [Celebrini] and make sure his movement is right," said Aaron Nelson, the head athletic trainer of Phoenix's well-respected training staff. "As soon as Steve begins feeling his shot is a little off, things can start happening. He's just very, very particular about everything. He really takes everything he does here on the [trainer's] table, in the weight room and on the court and makes sure his movement is right."

Nelson, a longtime fixture with the Suns, observed Nash's habits as both a rookie and a prized free agent and pronounced them "night-and-day different."

"He pays a lot more attention to what he eats and what he doesn't eat," Nelson said. "He's very particular. And with his conditioning he does everything he possibly can to keep his body right . . . A lot of people want to be stronger, they want to be faster. But the big thing for Steve and our staff is to be moving correctly, and he does everything so he's moving correctly on the court. So if he's going up for a shot and he's drifting a little bit—he'll know he's a little off; he'll feel different. I'm not aware of many people who pay that close attention to their mechanics on the court."

Indeed, while NBA teams have long employed shooting coaches to encourage players to improve their strokes in a way not dissimilar to golf professionals seeking expert advice on the practice tee, Nash essentially invented a new area of concentration: Celebrini came to be his shot mechanic. Although Nash, through observation and education, knows a thing or two about diagnosing the cause of any particular hiccup.

"If he's drifting [on his jumpshot] he might say his hips are out of line or his hamstrings are tight . . . he'll say maybe his glute medius isn't working or his left ankle is locked up," Nelson said. "Something [isn't right] . . . and he'll try to figure out what's causing that variation. He knows his body inside and out. We do manual therapy every day. He does his corrective exercises every day as mandated. He does absolutely everything. He really works hard. I'm not saying that because it sounds good.

He's one of the rare guys who, top to bottom, everything you can look at to make your body right, he does it."

He's rare because NBA workout rooms, as much as they're generally filled with strong men flexing impressive physiques, aren't always bastions of open-mindedness. Making the NBA, even for a gifted athlete, is an against-the-odds proposition; once a player makes it, it can be difficult for even the most persuasive voice to convince him to change the training methods that got him his multi-million-dollar salary and the life of privilege that came with it. Still, Nash's voice is more convincing than most. He has encouraged more than a few teammates to adopt some of his best practices, which have included post-exertion ice baths in 11°C water to reduce inflammation in his body, not to mention various forms of massage, the elimination of sugar from the diet and the keeping of a sleep journal. Some teammates have come to appreciate the usefulness of Nash's methods, even if reluctantly.

Witness Marcin Gortat, the Suns centre with a body-builder's chiselled frame and an Eastern European accent that roughly recalls Arnold Schwarzenegger: "I was like, shit, if Steve Nash is doing it, it can't be bad for me," Gortat said. "[At first] it was boring, I thought it was use-less. I love to lift big weights and they were not lifting big weights, that was the problem for me. So I thought in the beginning, 'What am I doing these girl's exercises for?' The leg lifting, it's girl stuff, like aerobics class. I'm like, 'How am I going to get better doing that? Let's go do some squats, some cleans, some bench press. Let's do some true freaking lifts,' you know?

"But Steve was like, 'You just got to do it, and after a

while you're going to get better. It's going to take time to get your rhythm, adjust your body to that kind of practice, but you're going to feel better. He was like, 'March . . . if you do it, you will play longer.' I started doing it and bam, I'm getting results . . . I'm not looking bad at all."

This was Nash in a nutshell: getting results without the big bang of barbell-bending weights or rim-wrecking slams. He's been called "unathletic." He's been referred to as an "average" athlete. And perhaps by some measures of jump-out-of-the-gym explosiveness, those terms could be considered accurate. But by so many other measures, Nash could only be considered an otherwordly athlete. He's been called the Bobby Fischer of basketball for a brain that appears to stay a move or two ahead of the other players on the hardwood chessboard. He's possessed of superior vision and timing and hand-eye genius that simply aren't seen in the typical pro.

Dick Davey, Nash's coach at Santa Clara, figures he could have been a pro in at least a few other sports if he'd so chosen; if Nash's soccer skills are well-known, less understood are his handiness with a baseball bat and a hockey stick. Taking batting practice with the San Francisco Giants at the invitation of Santa Clara teammate and long-time major leaguer Randy Winn back in 2006, Nash, who hadn't picked up a bat since he was about twelve, did a decent impression of a utility infielder, slashing some credible liners into the outfield before Willie Mays asked him for his autograph. ("I thought he was joking," Nash would say.) Nash gave up playing elite-level hockey around age thirteen to concentrate on basketball. He also showed promise in rugby.

And what of Nash's perceived lack of foot speed?

"Speed isn't the answer," Hubie Brown, the former NBA coach and longtime TV analyst, said. "All of the greatest passers are guys who are a half a step off the speed merchants. The speed merchants are out of control."

"The speed merchants," in Brown's view, are players with the kind of rare quickness that impresses fans and, at its best, can obliterate opponents. A 2010 *Sports Illustrated* poll of NBA players listed LeBron James as the fastest runner from baseline to baseline, while a selection of guards, among them Leandro Barbosa, Monta Ellis and Tony Parker, were among the top five. In a footrace with Nash, they'd all be a few steps ahead—maybe quite a few. But basketball is a team game, not a footrace. Change of pace is more important than flat-out speed. Stopping on a dime to make a jumpshot—one of Nash's great skills—is more important than starting with the ground force of an Olympic sprinter. And as for passing, Brown said, the greatest almost all have one thing in common. Brown listed off the likes of forwards LeBron James, Rick Barry, Charles Barkley and Larry Bird, not to mention point guards Magic Johnson and Nash himself. It was not, Brown said, his definitive list, but it was a telling one.

"Outside of LeBron James, they're all a half a step slow," Brown said. "They all play their game where they are seeing the floor, seeing the defence, seeing the offensive people moving. They are two clicks ahead of you, but they are constantly under control so that they can make the play. The speed aspect is not required because they read so well. They see everything in a different dimension than the masses do."

Between Nash's two MVP seasons and his eventual exit from Phoenix in 2012, the Suns made five runs to the post-season, three of which saw them reach the Western Conference final. In the early days, Phoenix was Nash's basketball Utopia, complete with an ideal coach and made-to-order teammates and a nice-guy franchise culture that suited its resident league MVP. But by the spring of 2010, Mike D'Antoni was gone, as was the "seven seconds or less" era. There had been myriad changes in Phoenix, where cost-conscious owner Robert Sarver took possession of the franchise in 2004 and Shaquille O'Neal ground the offence to a halt during a stopover that began in the lead-up to a first-round playoff ouster in 2007–08 and continued through a playoff-less 2008–09.

But after former D'Antoni assistant Alvin Gentry assumed the head-coaching position from the deposed Terry Porter, 2009–10 saw the Suns engineer what was perhaps their most unlikely trip to the doorstep of the NBA Finals. When Nash and the Suns found themselves down 2–0 to the Lakers in the 2010 Western final, they were counted out and promptly reeled off two straight wins. Nash was brilliant in Game 5, authoring a 29-point, 11-assist performance that was proven fruitless only after Ron Artest scored a buzzer-beating lay-in off a Kobe Bryant airball to win it for the Lakers. Nash caused something of a stir after that heart-busting loss by telling the cameras to be ready for Game 7, effectively guaranteeing the Game 6 victory. "That's no respect," a miffed Artest said. (Although other Lakers weren't at all perturbed by

Nash's comment: "What's he going to say?" said L.A. coach Phil Jackson, "'We're going to go home and lose'?")

The cameras were ready, but in the end they didn't need to be. Though in Game 6 it took Bryant 37 masterful points, 24 of which came in the second half, to outlast the Suns, who went into the fourth quarter of that decisive contest trailing by 17 and came within 3 points of the lead after a furious rally that recalled the best of their high-tempo high-wire act.

"Sometimes," Nash had said earlier in the series, "you just can't stop Kobe."

As Nash left the floor, he turned to applaud the Phoenix crowd.

"You want to say we overachieved until you think about it and say, 'We're a good team,'" Nash said. "You can maybe be greater than the sum of your parts. It was a lot of fun. I'd love to keep it together and keep going."

But the Phoenix machine had been going for a while, and never all the way to the intended destination. In 2005, Nash's first season back in Phoenix, the Suns had lost the Western final in five games to the San Antonio Spurs—this in the post-season that saw starting guard Joe Johnson break a bone near his eye that kept him out of the first two games of the series. Still, the season was an unequivocal success; there were experts who'd picked the Suns to barely finish above .500, let alone transform themselves into the highest-scoring unit the league had seen in a decade. And Nash, for his part, exacted some epic payback on the Mavericks by making a series of game-changing shots in Phoenix's six-game series win over Dallas in the Western semi-final. A snapshot of Nash's repeating brilliance came in the decisive Game 6 of that best-of-seven, wherein the Canadian made the three-pointer that forced overtime with 5.7 seconds to go before he made the three that sealed the game in the extra frame to finish with 39 points, 12 assists and 9 rebounds—a rebound short of his second straight triple-double.

"I think he really wanted to show all of Dallas what we missed [by not signing him as a free agent]," a stunned Dirk Nowitzki had said after Nash's performance, "and he really did that."

In 2006–07, after losing All-Star-in-waiting Johnson in a sign-and-trade deal to Atlanta that fetched centre-forward Boris Diaw, the Suns clawed their way to the Western final after they defeated all of Los Angeles—or, at least, both the Lakers and the Clippers—in back-to-back seven-game series in the first and second rounds, respectively. When Phoenix's NBAers arrived in pro basketball's version of the Final Four, where they met the Mavericks, they were weathered and worn. The injury-depleted Suns, by that point, were wobbling down the stretch with what amounted to a seven-man rotation. They'd already lost Stoudemire for the season to knee surgery in training camp. Raja Bell was playing on one leg. And still they built an 18-point lead on the Mavericks in Game 6, only to see foul trouble and fatigue lead to another season's demise.

"We're getting closer," Phoenix coach Mike D'Antoni said after it was over. But they actually wouldn't get any closer under D'Antoni. Nash would say later that the playoffs of 2007 represented Phoenix's best chance at a championship during his time with the franchise; that year the Spurs would go on to sweep a young LeBron

James and a thin Cleveland squad in an uneventful NBA Finals that spoke to the imbalance of power that resided out West. But that run saw the Suns suffer a memorable moment of NBA injustice. In a hotly contested Game 1 of the Western semi-final against the Spurs, Nash banged heads with San Antonio point guard Tony Parker to open a cut that left Nash on the bench at crunch time in a Phoenix loss. And when Nash was infamously hip-checked into the scorer's table by Robert Horry near the end of a Game 4 win by the Suns that tied the series 2–2, it was Nash's teammates who paid the price for coming to his defence. Stoudemire and Diaw were suspended a game apiece for coming off the Phoenix bench in the ensuing melee. Their absence in Game 5, won by the Spurs, argu-ably turned the tide of the series while turning the Suns into a team that will forever be remembered alongside a series of what-ifs.

What if Stoudemire had been healthy in 2006? What if those two playoff suspensions hadn't been doled out? What if they'd acquired a defensive-focused centre or simply spent a little more time focusing on defence? What if Sarver had been willing to spend enough to keep Johnson?

"I think if anything we proved to me that we can win a championship playing this way," said Nash. "I mean, for us to be as close as we are . . . with a six-, eight-man rotation [and injuries] . . . you can't tell me that we couldn't [have] won one of the close games, or two of these close games in the series. So, our feeling we can really win a championship playing this way? Definitely. If anything, this year went farther to convince me of that."

It wasn't to be. Despite that rebirth in 2010 under Gentry,

there was no stopping Kobe Bryant. When the Suns lost that year's Western final to Bryant and his Lakers, the NBA had a classic matchup on its hands, Lakers-Celtics clashing for the title. The Suns, meanwhile, were on the decline. By the beginning of the following season, Stoudemire, a free agent after the Suns' loss to L.A., would be playing in New York.

Nash, for his part, would stay in Phoenix with a gutted team. He didn't need to be reminded that his personal win-loss record in conference-final series had sunk to 0–4. He didn't need to be told that, for all his amazing achievements, he was at the time also the bearer of a less-than-desirable distinction: the only MVP never to play in the NBA Finals.

"I know everyone makes a deal out of I've never made the Finals," Nash said. "You know, maybe I won't. But if I played with teams like I played on this year, the guys I played with, you know, I'll be satisfied with that. It's phenomenally rewarding to be part of a group like this . . . This is about as special a group as I've ever been part of."

He also didn't need to be informed of a bit of stark reality: for all his blood, all his toil, all his no-stone-unturned training methods—for everything he'd given, his career might never get better than this. And with that, a former MVP was at peace.

CHAPTER SiX

From *No Logo* to Entrepreneur: The Twenty-Year Plan

Steve Nash couldn't contain himself.

He was sitting at a boardroom table surrounded by a trio of friends and business associates. They had fresh fruit on the table and pads of paper with pens at the ready, and a whiteboard for keeping track of numbers and ideas. They had gathered here in Phoenix to talk about the business they had just bought. Nash had convened the meeting, showing initiative that would have been unthinkable a decade before. He was known early in his NBA career as a peace-loving iconoclast who slouched around off the court in T-shirts, skateboard shoes and shaggy hair. Back then, profiles about him inevitably touched on his reading list, which included light lifting such as *The Communist Manifesto* and *No Logo* by Naomi Klein. And yet here he was in the spring of 2009, heading a group that had just been awarded an MLS expansion franchise worth $35 million. The trio of businessmen joining him were worth, collectively, well north of a billion dollars. There was Jeff Mallett, formerly of Yahoo! and a mentor to Nash in recent years. Also there was Greg Kerfoot, another successful tech entrepreneur, and Steve Luczo, a financier and part owner of the Boston Celtics. "Hey guys, you want to know something?" Nash began. "This is my first official board meeting and this is awesome!"

So began the Vancouver Whitecaps' first ownership meeting. The club's purchase was sparked, in a way, by a challenge Mallett had sent Nash not long after the two had reconnected on the Vancouver charity circuit shortly after Nash's first NBA All-Star game in 2003. Nash wanted to expand his charitable work but was beginning to understand that he would need to step outside his comfort zone to do it and was beginning to examine what that might mean. Mallet's premise was simple: It's twenty years from now. You have fifteen minutes to talk about what you've done after your playing career. If you mention basketball you fail.

"The email was really about what is the big idea germinating inside you," Mallett says.

It turned out that Nash had quite a few big ideas germinating inside him. And since the prod from Mallett, he's brought several to life. *Fast Company* magazine put Nash on the cover of their February 2010 issue and branded him the NBA's most successful entrepreneur. That may be debatable, but there's little question Nash is one of the most forward-thinking athletes anywhere when it comes to integrating his on-court persona with his off-court brand. He owns or co-owns the aforementioned soccer team, a film production company, a venture capital company, a chain of health clubs, a healthy fast-food franchise and a charitable foundation. He is the general manager of Canada Basketball's national men's team and endorses vitamins, skin-care products and cellphones, all while managing a high-profile, high-pressure job with the Los Angeles Lakers.

"It's very valuable to be doing this while I have the visibility of my career," Nash told Paul Coro of the *Arizona Republic* in 2009. "I'm at a stage of my life where I want to learn, grow and try different things. I get more life out of this than playing golf or other things athletes do in their spare time. This can stress me out, but it's also invigorating.

"I can't sit still. It'd be wonderful if I could. It sounds relaxing and a fun way to spend retirement, but it wouldn't work for me."

Nash's entrepreneurial ethos and willingness to leverage his own celebrity to his advantage weren't givens when he broke into the NBA. Even as he was beginning to make an impact with his play in Dallas alongside Dirk Nowitzki, he remained a reluctant public figure.

"It took a while for me to realize how really famous he was getting," says Greg Francis, a former national teammate who visited Nash periodically as his NBA star rose. "But I visited him in his last year in Dallas, and I met him after the game at a club and we were just sitting down and catching up and a group of people would come up and be like, 'Hey Steve' and as the night went on and on, groups of people would come up and he would accommodate all of them and still have a conversation with me. You could tell he was practiced at it. He would keep everyone happy and still have a conversation about old times, but I was like, 'Wow, this is different.'

"And when he got to Phoenix he got even bigger . . . he was on ESPN all the time, there's all this MVP talk. You'd go out with him there and he's like a rock star.

"He'll never tell you how big he is, but it's there."

Nash didn't disdain the attention that came with life in the public eye, but it was an adjustment. A friend described him as being deeply concerned with maintaining his core values while a celebrity culture swirled around him. Being famous challenged an ethic built on substance over style. How do you prove yourself as the underdog outsider when you're an A-list star? "I think he struggles, or at least struggled, with two things," the friend said. "One is why he is so fortunate and the other is what is his greater purpose in life? I think he feels guilty for living such a comfortable lifestyle and being born lucky. I think that is the reason he is an avid traveller and loves culture and language. He is trying to understand where he fits in the grand scheme of things and the NBA lifestyle is so superficial—although he has everything anyone could hope for, he isn't always at peace with himself or his situation."

Nash acknowledged the absurdity of being a constant centre of attention during the 2004–05 season, his first with Phoenix: "Sometimes it's hard to be normal, yeah, but you get used to it. The thing is you can go out and be normal with your friends, but inevitably, somewhere inside you, you know people are watching and recognize you. So you're trying to act normally, but you know you're trying to be normal, so it's not really normal. Eventually you just deal with it."

Helping Nash to acclimate himself to his growing celebrity was the good it allowed him to do. He describes his childhood in Victoria as overwhelmingly "normal," in a middle-class Canadian kind of way. But even as he spent so much of his waking energy pursuing his basketball dreams he was aware that experience—a loving, supportive family, lots of friends, chances to go to good schools and play all kinds of sports without overwhelming pressure—was more unusual than he would have liked to think. "You just realize there is a whole world of inequality out there," he explains. "And with that you develop the desire to be part of change and help people that need help."

The problem was how. Even in the early days of his professional career, long before he had signed contracts worth a total $150 million, he contributed his time and presence when asked. He made charitable donations, and sometimes he would just dig in his jeans and give some more, as when he treated his underfunded Olympic teammates to a shopping spree in the summer of 2000.

Nash's parents deserve some credit for influencing their son's value system. The Nashes lived in South Africa when Steve was born but left for Canada shortly thereafter, fed up with living under Apartheid. John Nash was a Tottenham Hotspur fan growing up; with the club's traditional ties to the Jewish community in London, "Spurs" were long a bastion of liberalism and tolerance. Young Steve would have fit right in. But even Nash's parents have been caught offguard by their son's generosity.

John Nash tells a story about where his son's head was at when he started making NBA money. When John moved to Victoria and began working for a local credit union, he set up within the business a formal charitable foundation. He served as the bookkeeper, fundraiser and grant provider.

"When I was at the credit union I used to keep a detailed record of the money we'd committed or given away, and I did the same for Stephen [in the early days of his charity work]. And I told him he'd given away $500,000 and I was expecting him to say, 'Holy shit, that's a lot of money.' And instead he said . . . 'Dad, think how much more we can give away to people less fortunate than us.' I had a lump in my throat the size of an apple. I was absolutely flabbergasted that this was my little boy. I was stunned almost. That was my proudest moment as a parent, almost. I don't think I would have given away the amount of money he's given away now. He's so committed."

When the Vancouver Grizzlies departed for Memphis after the 2000–01 season, they left in the lurch a minor basketball program the club had been sponsoring. Nash took over what is now Steve Nash Youth Basketball, a minor basketball association throughout British Columbia. Naming a kids' league after himself might make it seem like Nash had let his ability to help others go to his head, but the fact is that his father talked him into it, arguing that thousands of hoops-playing kids would be attracted to a league named after their hero. His son could hardly argue the logic, but it didn't mean he had to like it.

"I always wanted to do more, but I had two issues," Nash says. "One was that I felt really uncomfortable with getting attention, praise or credit for charity. I wrestled with that. I felt like it was almost distasteful."

The other, he says, was coming to grips with the nature of celebrity itself. Nash is aware that there is something strange—as Bruce Springsteen sang—about being paid a king's ransom for doing what comes naturally, but at a certain point you just have to roll with it.

"It would be sad and a bit wasteful to say 'this is silly' all day long," he says. "If you use it to be positive and accept it, then it's not as silly anymore, or at least it doesn't have the same silly effect on you."

Accepting his own celebrity seems to have allowed Nash to give all of himself to his charitable endeavours. Steve Nash Basketball has since gone national. The program is administered by Canada Basketball as a turnkey community initiative to bring the sport to kids aged 9 through 13, not that different than Pop Warner football or Babe Ruth League in the United States, with the differentiating bonus being that the program's namesake may drop in on a clinic every once in a while to pat heads the way only a living legend can.

His instinctual need to use his good fortune to help others has matured from digging into his pockets and giving away money to building and staffing his own charitable foundation and leveraging his celebrity to help raise money in a more effective way. He hired a lawyer and family friend, Jenny Miller, to run the foundation full-time, and also brought his sister, Joann, on board. In 2005, the newly formed Steve Nash Foundation had its first high-profile public fundraiser, the Steve Nash Foundation Charity Classic, held at a nearly sold-out Air Canada Centre on a mid-summer's night in Toronto. Fellow Victoria make-good story, Grammy-winner Nelly Furtado, was the halftime entertainment and a handful of NBA stars participated, but Nash was the centre of attention, whether it was teaming for alley-oops with the high-flying Andre

Iguodala or allowing himself to be schooled by a pint-sized ball-handling impresario. It was Nash's name that had encouraged a major cellphone company to sign on as a presenting sponsor. It was his presence that drew media coverage and his causes were the ones benefitting from the effort. Finally Nash was able to accept being fussed over. "It's never the easiest thing in the world, for me, to be complimented in front of other people," Nash said. "I'd rather keep a low profile, but if I can give back to the community and that's the cost, I can do that."

Since that first event in 2005, the guy who read *No Logo* has found increasingly creative ways to turn his name recognition into a weapon for positive change. After holding a few charity basketball games, Nash came up with a new centrepiece event that capitalized on his soccer-loving roots called Showdown in Chinatown, a pick-up game held on a small-sided field in Manhattan's Chinatown that coincides with the NBA draft. With key national media figures on hand and a funky, grassroots feel, the event always gets its share of coverage, and seeing as it's held in New York and around a big event on the league calendar, it's easier for Nash to lasso fellow NBA stars into participating—a challenge akin to herding cats if there ever was one (Nash's basketball events in Toronto and Vancouver were undermined to some degree each year by notable no-shows). And Nash's soccer bona fides mean he can tap into some high profile international stars of the Beautiful Game, like former Arsenal striker and MLS New York Red Bulls star Thierry Henry, who look forward to the chance to rub shoulders with some NBA stars.

Over the years Showdown—as it's now called, with a second game happening in Los Angeles each year—has become the signature Steve Nash event: it's full of celebrities but free of the pretension of a gala. It involves getting all sweaty doing something they're not necessarily good at: image-conscious Miami Heat star Chris Bosh had never played soccer before he suited up for Showdown. And it's free to the public, raising money through sponsorships instead of ticket sales.

Nash remains the driving force behind his foundation, and often its main source of funds. In addition to Showdown, he can count among a series of successes a post-operative pediatric cardiology ward at Hospital de Clínicas in Asunción, Paraguay—his ex-wife's hometown—as well as more than $650,000 in grants to programs aimed at under-serviced children in his home province of B.C. But an interesting thing happened to Nash as his charitable motives pushed him to embrace the value of his own name and cultivate relationships with those in business and power: he began to get curious about business and more comfortable with the idea of a career that didn't revolve around basketball.

It was a significant transformation, better understood with a look at just how improbable it would have seemed earlier in his career. When Nash showed up at the ballroom of the Omni Hotel in downtown Atlanta for his first NBA All-Star weekend in 2003, it's fair to say he stood apart from his peers. In those days—before NBA commissioner David Stern invoked his infamous dress code—most gatherings of NBA players looked like rap videos, with layers of jewelry draped over throwback jerseys. Nash walked in wearing jeans, sneakers and a simple green T-shirt reading:

"No War, Shoot for Peace." At the time it didn't cause a huge stir. Nash was primarily the focus of a small handful of Canadian reporters, and given the Canadian government was only a few weeks away from officially declaring that they would not join American action against Iraq, pacifism wasn't viewed as a particularly radical position.

But for a Canadian basketball star playing in Dallas, Texas, it was notable. Nash had decided to wear the T-shirt after Hemsa Nosh, a friend from his high school days in Victoria and a part of the burgeoning peace movement at UBC, helped him better understand opposition to the war.

"We're catching up one day and he asked what I was doing and I was at UBC and had gotten really inspired with a student group at UBC and the anti-war movement," his friend Nosh said. "We . . . talked for about an hour and he asked a lot of questions. He was like, 'I really, really, want to do something . . . I'm going to the All-Star Game next week, can you send me a shirt? I'll stand up for this.'

"We had to get one made . . . the T-shirts we had were a little more radical—'No Blood for Oil' wasn't him—so a friend came up with 'No War, Shoot for Peace,' and I think it was perfect."

While Nash's first political statement wasn't exactly Muhammad Ali declaring, "I ain't got no quarrel with them Viet Cong. No Viet Cong ever called me nigger," it was something. Ali was stripped of his heavyweight belt and sentenced to prison for refusing to serve in the Vietnam War; Nash was hardly a zealot—he still drove a gas-chugging Range Rover at the time. But in an era when athletes were racing to "Be Like Mike"—smoothing away unpopular personal principles as Michael Jordan had in the race to cash in with corporate sponsors—that Nash was willing to say anything that required him to answer potentially difficult questions made him unique. "Speaking out about something other than the game is something sports figures in this country run from, especially if the topic is something so controversial it is dividing a nation and the world," wrote *Dallas Morning News* columnist Kevin Blackistone. "For those athletes who aren't so ignorant to what is going on outside their gated homes, the fear of alienating the ticket-buying, sneaker-wearing public is too great to share any serious thoughts.

"Refreshingly, Nash has chosen a different path, like Arthur Ashe and Muhammad Ali and a few others before him. He's a new iconoclast for the new millennium."

Nash wasn't entirely alone: Mavericks teammate Nick Van Exel mused on a Dallas radio station shortly after war was declared on Iraq that it could end up embarrassing the U.S. and giving the country a "bad name" internationally. But Nash was certainly the only All-Star making a statement.

Fellow NBA All-Star David Robinson of the rival San Antonio Spurs, a former officer in the U.S. Navy, was among the voices critical of Nash's anti-war stance. "The time for debate is really beforehand. Obviously history will speak on whether this was the right thing or the wrong thing, but right now [the soldiers] are out there. Support 'em. There's plenty of time for commentary later.

"If it's an embarrassment to [Nash and Van Exel]," Robinson added, "maybe they should be in a different country, because this is America and we're supposed to be proud of the guys we elected and put in office."

Nash stood firm, telling Marc Stein of ESPN: "From the start, I spoke out just because I don't want to see the loss of life. People are mistaking anti-war as being unpatriotic. This has nothing to do with the fact that I'm from Canada. This is a much bigger issue. But now that we're in battle, I hope for as many lives to be spared as possible, [and] as little violence as possible before a resolution . . .

"I never said, 'Go out and believe what I believe.' [The message] was, 'Go out and decide for yourself.' But I am 100 percent behind the soldiers protecting our freedom. Who wouldn't be?

"I'm not embarrassed by America," Nash said. "I'm embarrassed by humanity. More than embarrassed, I think it's really unfortunate in the year 2003 that we're still using violence as a means of conflict resolution. That's what I'm speaking out against."

A decade later and Nash's first peek into political activism remains his most notable one. The guy who spoke out about the war, read *No Logo* and was basketball's grungy, hipster superstar is pushing forty now and has started his tenure in L.A. sporting a brush cut. His foundation is well established and his Showdown has gone bicoastal. But at this age, the day twenty years in the future that Mallet challenged him to think about, is looking closer all the time.

He took that email from Mallett to heart. Nash, the guy who was reluctant to put himself out in the public eye, realized that it's not so bad, all things considered, and if he's out there anyway, he might as well use the power of his profile to help him fill those fifteen minutes.

———

The same qualities that have made Nash a surefire Hall of Famer have set him up for what appears to be a second act that, not inconceivably, could match his first. "I've seen a lot of athletes come and go so I can filter things and see through guys pretty quickly," said Mallett. "We [were] at a fundraiser in Victoria, having a beer, staring over the water, just BS'ing and it could have been just 'have fun, shake hands and move on,' but I had a dialogue with him and he was very curious about Yahoo! and what was that like and how do you create media and a business, so he was asking me in a non-business situation—it wasn't inappropriate— but it wasn't a business situation and he asked me very insightful questions in a manner that wasn't small talk and it really struck me that this is different than just another brand icon; this is someone who really asks questions and more importantly really listens carefully to the answers."

Clearly. As of this writing Nash's financial interests include a portfolio of investments that fit in with an over- all brand strategy centred on sports, health and wellness. Among them are Liquid Nutrition, a Montreal-based, quick-serve health food restaurant chain and OneBode, a Phoenix-based vitamin and supplement manufacturer and retailer specializing in plant-based products. Then there's a chain of eighteen fitness centres in B.C. that bears his name (Steve Nash Sports Clubs) and a pair of projects particularly close to his heart: his founding stake in the Vancouver Whitecaps—the subject of that first-ever board meeting in Phoenix—and co-ownership of Meathawk, a film production company he started with his cousin, Ezra Holland. He also does more traditional celebrity endorse- ments with the likes of Bridgestone Tires, Dove Men+Care,

Chinese sportswear manufacturer Luyou and Sprint. He also has a stake in a small venture capital company, Consigliere Brand Capital. All of his holdings operate under the umbrella of Steve Nash Enterprises, which is led by Brandon Kou, a youthful business school graduate from Los Angeles whose primary wish, as Nash tries to navigate his multiple business partnerships and his career, is to "clone him."

Seems like a lot to have been set in motion by a single email.

"That's how it all started to come about," says Mallett.

Following Mallett's challenge, Nash met with Jenny Miller from his foundation, Bill Duffy, his agent, and Mallett over a weekend in the Napa Valley and came up with the bones of the Steve Nash brand.

"We sketched some stuff down and it's been the template that he's used with regard to his foundation and health and fitness, his media, which he really, truly enjoys," continues Mallet. "He likes original ideas, he likes to produce it, he likes to act in it—and we put all that together and hired Brandon Kou out of Los Angeles to help make it real.

"The result is he's set up to have a nice post-basketball career that's already in place before he steps off the hardwood."

As a philanthropist and entrepreneur, Nash has come a long way, but the evolution fits with Nash's overall profile.

"He was always determined and positive and it hasn't changed," Hemsa Nosh, the high school friend turned peace activist says. "He was the type of person who believed that whatever you put your mind to you could achieve, that's what made him stand out. He had this drive and this super-positive attitude . . . I remember him teaching me to shoot baskets and he was like 'you can do it, it's just a matter of visualizing it' . . . to hear that from a seventeen-year-old stood out. I tell him all the time, out of everyone I know, he deserves what he's got and the success he's had."

He may just be getting started. In a profile in the business magazine *Forbes*, he cited Lakers legend Magic Johnson as a role model, not because they both rank in the top five of all time in NBA assists, but because Johnson's been nearly as successful an entrepreneur as he was a basketball player.

But even as the fields change, what Nash brings to the situation is often similar to what he does on the court. On the floor, the Steve Nash brand has stood for finding rhythm amidst the chaos and managing to impose inno- cent, almost childlike values—teamwork, trust, spontane- ity and fun—into the too-often self-interested world of professional basketball. Nash's truest gift is overcoming that cynicism time and time again. It's a remarkable feat. That quality, in simple terms, is empathy. He understands what his teammates need and why, and does his best to make it so. "He's constantly trying to learn and trying to grow and trying to love, that's the bottom line," says his former Olympic teammate and friend Rowan Barrett. "He's one of the most giving, open-minded guys I've ever met. If you really understand the game, it's really easy to understand what he's like, I mean, he's constantly trying to give the ball away, he's running around, dribbling, cut- ting, slashing, tiring himself out just so he can go 'here's the ball.' He makes it easy for you."

In that context, given Nash's inventiveness with a bas- ketball in his hands, it shouldn't be surprising that the project closest to his heart is one that engages his creative impulses.

By the summer of 2007 Nash was at his peak as a basketball player, and was ready to delve into other interests. His wife at the time, Alejandra, was the daughter of a film buff and helped pique Nash's interest in the medium. The following summer he and his cousin Ezra Holland pitched the idea of filming an online video about his off-season training routine to Nike.

The result was "Training Day." The video features Nash riding his skateboard between solo basketball workouts in the parks of New York City, as well as goofing around with tennis and pick-up soccer. Spliced in are some home movies of him playing soccer as a kid in Victoria.

Nash does the voiceover, talking in an understated way about how soccer has influenced the way he plays on the court: "It's such a creative outlet to try to encompass all those different moving parts . . . the passion and appreciation for the finer points of soccer easily translated into basketball."

Nash's appreciation for the synchronized chaos of sport translated into the visual arts too. His low-key presentation in video fit perfectly with both his overall image and the explosion of self-produced content online. "Training Day" went viral and has since received more than 500,000 views on YouTube; not bad for a $30,000 investment by Nike.

The success of that video inspired Nash and Holland to form Meathawk. Their first collaboration was another commercial for Nike called "The Sixty Million Dollar Man." In it Nash makes like Steve Austin in the 1970s television hit *The Six Million Dollar Man* and is rebuilt from recycled parts—a reasonably subtle way for Nike to introduce their new Trash Talk shoe—a basketball sneaker made of recycled rubber. Several lighter-hearted videos followed depicting life on the Phoenix Suns' plane, all of which pointed towards Nash gaining confidence as a performer, building a brand of deadpan humour and proving the value that Meathawk could provide for companies that wanted to do business with him. When he began endorsing Vitaminwater, Nash helped conceive and produce their online advertising. The YouTube spots that resulted starred Nash as The Spokesman, striding through Vitaminwater head office playing the role of an obliviously pompous pitchman or preparing for a photo shoot and uttering lines such as, "I hear people talk about me so much and I forget—I really am great" and "I'm just like you, just ten times better." It's fun stuff, and it works.

"At some point, you cross the line from being a spectator to participant," was how Nash described the evolution. "It just sort of happened as innocently as that and keeps moving.

"That need to be creative and get things off your chest—to express things—is fulfilling, much [like] basketball."

YouTube endorsements were one thing, but when Nash was approached by the production arm of ESPN about participating in *30 for 30*, the documentary series designed to celebrate the thirtieth anniversary of the culture-defining sports network, he knew it was a chance he had to take. And he knew exactly the thing he wanted to share with the world.

It says much about Nash that perhaps the moment when all he hoped to stand for came together not in a boardroom, but in a graveyard in Port Coquitlam, B.C. It was June 28, 2009, and the beer and wine were flowing on a warm summer's night. Nash's unlikely basketball journey—from obscurity to fame around the world; from an athlete with a social conscience to an entrepreneur with a vision—had brought him to the grave of a young man whose story perhaps most fully illuminates Nash's own attributes and growing passions. He and a group of filmmakers were gathered on the 28th anniversary of the untimely death of Terry Fox, the 21-year-old who galvanized a nation—including a 6-year-old Steve Nash—with the Marathon of Hope, Fox's magnificent attempt to run across Canada in the summer of 1980 to raise money and awareness for cancer research. Coincidentally, Fox had been an award-winning basketball player in high school, a starting guard no less, and was playing for Simon Fraser University when cancer shut down his season and necessitated the amputation of his right leg above the knee. Images of his determined one-legged hop along lonely highways are iconic to Canadians. Nash identified with Fox's journey so powerfully that even as his interests beyond basketball grew, he was drawn inexorably back to the story of a B.C. kid who took on the disease that cost him a limb and, ten months after forcing him off the road almost halfway across Canada, his life. Nash had the profile because of his own journey and chose to use it to tell the world the story of someone who had inspired him.

He and Holland would introduce Terry Fox to the United States.

Selling ESPN was a breeze, as Nash and Holland got the project green-lighted on the strength of a single meeting. There were no proposals exchanged, just some conversation and a handshake—the perks of being a celebrity.

"Of course, that's how it is, right?" Nash deadpanned at

a press conference during the Toronto International Film Festival. "You tell people what you're going to do and they give you money to do it, right?"

No doubt attaching Nash's name to the project didn't hurt, but it was his passion for the story that ultimately came through.

"I got a chance to approach ESPN on the project and I think that a big part of them going for it was I told them that I woke up every day as a six-year-old that summer and turned on the TV to find out where Terry was to watch him run across our country," Nash explained on *30 for 30*, executive producer Bill Simmons' podcast. "You couldn't think of a more boring thing to do, but we were riveted. We were glued to it because he was such an inspirational figure. He was so selfless and humble and uncompromising. Just an incredible person. He's one of my heroes and had an impact on how I live my life as an athlete and why I have my own charitable foundation."

There remains an innocent sense of wonder that touches all Nash does, and if there's a lesson to be gleaned from his own journey it might be: evolve, but don't change. Basketball, the way Nash plays it, is deeply collaborative, spontaneous and an outlet for both his creative and competitive sides. Outside of basketball, Nash has sought to stick to that script.

CHAPTER SEVEN

L.A. Confrontational: Lost in Lotusland

With a route as long and winding and unprecedented as Steve Nash's path to the peak of professional basketball, you have to be careful when trying to suggest something has come full circle. Where did the circle begin, after all? Was it in the backyard playing footie with his dad, John, and brother, Martin, where his dad would encourage the boys to look for each other, taking the ball off them when they played selfishly—Nash's first lesson in finding the open man? Was it in Grade 8 when his buddies were getting serious about basketball and he decided he'd better, too, if he wanted to keep up? Was it his early national team experiences or his first NBA training camp?

Just as difficult is determining where the circle closes. Nash returning to Victoria to accept an honorary degree from UVic with a pair of NBA MVP awards to his name would be a great place to finish any doting biopic. Similarly,

Nash taking the helm of Canada Basketball, bringing order and credibility and hope to the organization that shaped his own ambitions, would make for good final act.

But the argument here for full circle closure came when the clock struck midnight on July 1, 2012, signalling the start of the NBA's free agency period. After eight years running with the Suns (not counting the two he spent in the desert to start his career), Nash was no longer under contract in Phoenix. The Suns had just missed the playoffs for the second straight year, unable to follow up their remarkable run to the Western Conference finals in 2010. By the 2011–12 season, the writing was on the wall: it was time for the Suns to get over their Steve Nash dependency, and for Nash to find a way to end his NBA career in style.

Even if Nash had decided to leave the game at that moment, he was heading to Springfield and the Basketball Hall of Fame. But Nash wasn't ready to walk away.

"I enjoy it," he offered, after another loss in Phoenix during his final season there. "One, it's a pretty good job. Two, there's going to be a long stretch of my life, hopefully, where I don't play—hopefully I'm alive a long time. I still have a passion for it, not only for the competition and the challenge, but also for the lifestyle. It's great to train every day. I enjoy being fit and well and challenging myself.

"And the biggest thing is to look at the flip side: If I wasn't playing, what would I be doing and how would it stack up to this? It's hard to compare something with going and playing hoops with a bunch of guys every day and going and competing against the best guys in the world."

But wanting to stay in the league and still being able to at age thirty-eight are two different things. So what happened to Nash after the clock struck midnight. Did Cinderella have to leave the ball? Did the carriage turn into a pumpkin? Was Nash on the outside looking in as the free agent carousel began to turn?

Quite the opposite. Steve Nash was the apple in the eye of some of the NBA's most successful franchises. Two decades after leaving Victoria to begin his basketball odyssey, Nash was a wanted man and poised to ascend to the stars.

Before beginning the next—and likely final—chapter of his storybook career, Nash had to make a graceful exit from the orbit of the Phoenix Suns. The price of his success in the desert was that he was now inextricably linked—at least in the public eye—with the image of him racing around in a Suns jersey, No. 13. And loyalty was inextricably linked to any image of Nash.

As much as he worked his way into the fabric of the desert city during his MVP years, Nash may have endeared himself even more in the ones that followed. There was little doubt that the Suns were changing under the ownership of Robert Sarver, who had bought the team from Jerry Colangelo, one of the modern NBA's founding fathers and the man who brought Nash to Phoenix. Piece by piece the masterful mosaic that was the "seven seconds or less" Suns was being dismantled. In the summer of 2010, after Phoenix lost the Western Conference finals in six games to the heavily favoured Los Angeles Lakers, the team's other signature player, Amar'e Stoudemire, walked to the New York Knicks as a free agent. That the Suns allowed him to leave without putting up a fight sent a clear message: they were rebuilding.

Stoudemire's departure presented a perfect opportunity for Nash to discreetly ask out. And if the discreet inquiries weren't taken seriously, then he could stand up in the middle of the Suns' dressing room and scream, "Trade Me!"

Nash did neither. He didn't have to, really. His admirers were doing it for him. By the middle of the 2011–12 season there had emerged the #freestevenash hashtag on Twitter and a semi-serious Facebook campaign, complete with "Free Steve Nash" T-shirts. The aim of both campaigns was to encourage the Suns to allow Nash to go to a team with a chance to compete for an NBA championship, the only entry missing on his basketball resume.

Nash didn't bite, however. While everyone else seemed to want him to force his way out, he stayed the course.

"I really appreciate that," he said of the desire among fans [and some media] across the league to see him on a winning team. "They want me to succeed and do well and win a championship and be on a contender and that's great. But on the flip side . . . it's not my style to ask for a trade, for one, and two I feel like I'd be giving up on my teammates and we've had a lot of success here and for me, when the ship starts to sink a little bit, to be the first one off? I don't feel that comfortable with that."

It was, in retrospect, a masterstroke of public relations, sincerely and smoothly applied on a career canvas full of them, and delivered in a Suns locker room full of players whose time in the NBA will be relatively brief and mostly forgettable. But Nash's public statement of loyalty was a sign that he was willing to follow through on his beliefs even if they were detrimental in the short-term.

The biggest winners in the NBA are those teams that

actually play as a team. It seems obvious, but it makes the league inherently dramatic because nearly every circumstance in professional sports works against a group of players actually acting that way. In some ways the tension between what's good for the team and the organization and what is best for an individual in any given moment is the secret source of energy that makes the NBA go around.

"The contracts are structured in a way to benefit individuals with good statistics and good numbers. It takes a special player to realize if we stick together and play together we'll win and we'll all benefit, but not everyone has that attitude," says Todd MacCulloch, Nash's former national team teammate who played four years in the NBA before a rare nerve condition ended his career. "In college you're all playing together for the same goal. In the NBA everyone's got their contract coming up at different times and it can really change the dynamic. Everyone is out for their own—and in basketball one player can really take over the game on both ends and the NBA has always loved its stars—and sometimes guys' egos get in the way and it comes at the expense of teams.

"In the pros it's hard to get that kind of cohesiveness. It takes a special GM or coach or player to get over that because it's not a game on paper, it's a game with a lot of chemistry and everyone who has played with Steve knows he's going to make people better."

That ability to bring out the best in his teammates has been a part of Nash's game throughout his career and at every level. But the problem with making your mark as one of basketball's most unselfish and loyal players is that you risk that valuable image when you decide to put your own needs first and leave town. The NBA as a whole was taking a beating on the loyalty front as Nash's free agency approached. The summer of 2010 had borne witness to "The Decision," LeBron James's ill-advised ESPN special announcing his choice to leave his hometown Cleveland Cavaliers for the Miami Heat. It will probably go down as the most tin-eared public relations move in modern celebrity athlete culture, which is saying something. Chris Bosh, James's Heat teammate, generated some vitriol of his own when he asked for fan input on Twitter before eventually spurning the Raptors for the Heat and then going on to complain about the hardships of living in the NBA's only Canadian city, in particular enduring a subpar cable TV package. He was kidding, but it made him look terrible and turned Raptors fans against Bosh even more.

NBA superstars plotting their way out of town spread like a rash. Carmelo Anthony waged a year-long campaign to get out of Denver; Dwight Howard forever tarnished what was a charming image of a goofball kid trapped in a superhero's body when he campaigned to get his coach fired in Orlando before leaving the Magic with no option other than to trade him to the Los Angeles Lakers. Chris Paul declared that he wasn't going to resign with the league-owned New Orleans Hornets, forcing the wards of the NBA to trade him to the Los Angeles Clippers. So Nash staying true to the Suns until the not-bitter-at-all end was like adding grass seed to an already well-manicured lawn in a neighbourhood filled with over-grown yards overrun by weeds: he didn't need to burnish his image, but it certainly helped. Which isn't to suggest it was a contrivance, but simply an example of how far common sense and staying true to solid core values can take you in modern celebrity culture.

"In some ways there was a time where we were kicking everyone's butt everyday," Nash said when the Free Steve Nash drumbeat began to sound. "We didn't win a championship, but we weren't really built for a championship. So, in some ways the mentality is you have to take your lumps now and scrap out every win. I'm not necessarily embracing that, but it's a cyclical business and we're going through a bit of a down cycle—and you got to fight and see what you can do to get us back and any measure of improvement or exceeding expectations or being better than the sum of our parts is good as well.

"A lot of people seem to think it's a pretty foolish way to look at things," he said. "There's a lot of factors involved, but I'm not on the side of walking upstairs and saying trade me, we're not good enough."

That unselfishness is increasingly seen as a tragic flaw in a winner-take-all world where secondary players fortunate enough to be in the right place at the right time to contribute to winning teams—witness Robert Horry's seven NBA championship rings—are 'winners' and Hall of Famers such as Charles Barkley, Karl Malone and John Stockton are somehow diminished because they left the NBA ringless. Nash wasn't going to play that game.

"I don't feel like I need justification [that supposedly comes with winning an NBA ring]," he said. "I know what I can do. I know that I'm a great competitor and basketball player. Don't get me wrong, I'd love to have a shot at it and I believe that I still could, but now isn't the time to start demanding trades."

It's that attitude that explains the company Nash still keeps in the pub at Phoenix's Sky Harbor Airport. Only two sports jerseys hang on the pub's walls, both emblematic of certain levels of selflessness. One belongs to Pat Tillman, the former star with Arizona State and the NFL's Arizona Cardinals who retired from football to enlist in the U.S. Army after 9/11 and was killed in a tragic and controversial friendly fire incident in 2004. The other is the No. 13 Suns jersey that will forever belong to Nash.

Dwane Casey had seen this movie before, but the set was never as lavish, the stakes not nearly as high, and the money wasn't upfront. The Toronto Raptors head coach had arrived in the lush Park Avenue condominium belonging to Larry Tanenbaum, who had gone to the trouble of whisking Casey by private jet from the wedding of an assistant coach on the other side of the continent so he could help make a sales pitch. The Raptors' minority owner and their second-year head coach were part of a seven-man full-court press on a mission to convince Canada's only NBA star to come home. Casey had broken into coaching with the University of Kentucky, and knew what it meant to be "good in the kitchen"—the kind of coach who can make an impression on a key recruit while visiting with his family. Trying to recruit a high-profile NBA free agent was different, to be sure. Instead of his parents, Nash was accompanied by his long-time agent, Bill Duffy, and his girlfriend, Brittany Richardson. And he wasn't a high school hotshot, but a sixteen-year NBA veteran who had earned more than $100 million in his career and had spent the previous night in his own Manhattan pied-à-terre in SoHo, an easy commute uptown for the mid-morning meeting.

"We put together a presentation that was very impressive to Steve," says Casey. "It was an effort to show him how much we wanted him in our program. It reminded me of my recruiting visits when I was at Kentucky, going into homes and meeting families and things like that. It was a first-class presentation and we let him know what he would mean to the organization.

The centrepiece was a DVD narrated by none other than Wayne Gretzky, the Canadian hockey icon and one of Nash's idols growing up. The premise was that Nash coming home to play in Canada would have the same impact on basketball that Gretzky going to the Los Angeles Kings from the Edmonton Oilers in the famous 1988 trade had on the NHL's expansion into non-traditional hockey markets. The Raptors, four years removed from the playoffs with a 23–33 record to show for the lockout-shortened season, couldn't promise Nash a shot at the championship ring he'd missed out on in Dallas and Phoenix. Instead they were tugging at Nash's patriotic heartstrings and the opportunity to grow a profile beyond the floor.

"If Steve is going to retire, then what better place than here, in Canada?" says Tanenbaum, who led the presentation. From Olympic hero to national team general manager to Raptors éminence grise — attracting Nash to Toronto was part of a long-term play.

It was GM Bryan Colangelo, aided by Tanenbaum, who'd thought of reaching out to Gretzky for help with the recruitment video. "The idea was to get two Canadian icons together," said Tanenbaum. "The icon of Canadian hockey and the icon of basketball. I thought it was a brilliant move. Wayne did a spectacular job." Duffy later told Marc Stein of ESPN.com that the presentation moved Nash nearly to tears.

The meeting lasted the better part of two hours, but it wasn't a negotiation. Money wasn't really discussed, though the Raptors were willing to spend more than any other team for Nash's services, eventually offering a deal widely reported to be worth $36 million over three years. Beyond money, what was needed was a meeting of hearts and minds, and the Raptors gave it their best shot. Along with Gretzky on the video, Colangelo, Casey and Tanenbaum, Jay Triano, the former Raptors head coach and then scout who would soon leave for a position with the Portland Trail Blazers, made the trip, as did Jonny Lee, the Raptors' strength and conditioning coach and a close friend of Nash's from their days with the Canadian national team.

"We all felt good; it felt like family," said Tanenbaum. "It's not a negotiation, it's an expression not only of the interest we have in him, but why it's good, why it would be good for him, why it would be good for the team. We shared the culture of the organization, our priorities, our values. He wanted to hear about that. It was about building the building blocks in the case for him to come to Toronto. It's the building of the story and that takes time."

At the end of the meeting Nash expressed sincere thanks and then headed out for his next appointment; his day of being wooed was just getting started. After a limousine ride to a nearby heliport he was met by New York Knicks forward Carmelo Anthony and taken to the Knicks' practice facility north of the city, where every television set in the building was tuned in to the Euro 2012 final between Spain and Italy, a personal touch meant to impress the noted soccer fanatic. After that, it was another helicopter ride and a two-hour meeting with Knicks owner James Dolan on Dolan's yacht; about as far from an afternoon sitting with Jay Triano at Tsawwassen Ferry Terminal as you can get.

There were other overtures. The defending champion Miami Heat checked in. They couldn't come close to matching the money that the Raptors were offering but they did see Nash as someone that could help solidify a championship lineup, which was flattering. The New Jersey Nets were also interested, and the Los Angeles Lakers had made inquiries, even though Nash had said that years as a Sun banging heads against the Lakers made teaming up with them hard to imagine. Plus there was Kobe Bryant, Nash's long-time rival, who made clear that he didn't hold much affection for the Suns and their superstar point man. "I don't like them," Bryant said after a 2011 game in which he scored 48 points. It was one in a run of high-scoring games he hung on Phoenix, perhaps as payback for Nash snatching two MVP awards that Bryant surely felt he had claim to. "Plain and simple, I do not like them. They used to whip us pretty good and used to let us know about it, and I. Will. Not. Forget. That."

But the Lakers offered Nash something no other team could: the chance to win and, more importantly, the chance to stay within a reasonable commute of his three children in Phoenix.

In the lead-up to free agency Nash hadn't thought his children would have such an impact on his decision-making. Nash had been married to Alejandra Amarilla since 2005; the couple had twin daughters in October of 2004. The couple had a son in October of 2010 but announced their divorce the following day. It appeared amicable and Nash was an involved father, occasionally relating parenting moments via Twitter. But he maintained that he was prepared to work and live apart from his family in Phoenix if it meant securing a favourable final contract.

"Obviously you want to be with your kids," he said. "I have my kids whenever I'm home. I have a 50/50 custody arrangement and during the season that means whenever I'm home they're with me and in the summer it's 50/50. I don't want to not be here because [time with the kids] is very valuable to me, but I'm not going to make that the only factor or the biggest factor in whatever happens in any decision. I want to be really open in what happens and what transpires."

But the possibility of moving to Toronto or New York while his kids stayed behind turned out to be another thing altogether. As the summer wore on, the prospect of seeing his children only three or four times throughout the seven-month NBA season became tougher to face.

"He was going to retire," says Duffy. "He didn't want to leave his children."

The challenge then became to facilitate a best-of-both-worlds arrangement with the Lakers, where Nash could be within an hour's flight of his home in Phoenix and— whether the hard edges of the old rivalry wore down or not— a teammate of Kobe Bryant's. Left out in the cold were the Knicks and the Raptors. As the hours stretched to days with no word, it was becoming clear that Toronto had been reduced to a fallback plan.

Four days later the Lakers had their man. But only after Nash himself had appealed to Suns owner Robert Sarver.

He asked his boss to see beyond his obvious reluctance to deal the most popular player in franchise history to a division rival; to recognize that Nash had never stepped a foot wrong in his eight years with the franchise; and to focus on the assets he'd receive in return who could help Phoenix rebuild. In the end decency and common sense prevailed, and on July 12 Nash found himself at a press conference at the Lakers' El Segundo practice facility. Looking out on a sea of media, he summed it up as best he could, having just been handed a No. 10 Lakers home jersey with his name on it—the team's iconic No. 13 jersey was retired, with no less than Wilt Chamberlain's name on it. "It's a step I didn't foresee, it's surreal," said Nash, "but it's also exciting."

Exciting it may have been, but it was also the stiffest professional challenge that Nash had ever faced, and the ultimate test of everything he stood for as a basketball player.

It was the end of a road trip in the middle of a season that had already gone far wrong, at least compared to the beginning of the great experiment, when Nash was posed on the cover of *Sports Illustrated* with the other newest Laker, Dwight Howard, and the headline: "This Is Going to Be Fun!" The trip had started with a bittersweet return to Phoenix. Nash was recognized with a video tribute and the Suns fans, rather than resenting him for decamping to the Lakers, chose to honour him for his time in the desert. The Lakers paid them back for their thoughtfulness, blowing a 13-point fourth-quarter lead to the lottery-bound Suns. As the trip wore on, nerves got frayed and as things tend to in Laker-land, it spilled over publicly.

It had been a trying season from the start. With a lineup featuring six players with a combined thirty-five All-Star appearances among them, the expectation was that the Lakers would be very good, very early. As soon as they stuggled, patience was in short supply. After the team went 0–8 in the pre-season and then started the regular season 1–4 and was still slogging through the installation of the Princeton offence—a motion-based approach that was itself an odd choice given the pick-and-roll abilities of Nash as a point guard—the Lakers fired incumbent coach Mike Brown.

And while things improved under his replacement, Mike D'Antoni—Nash's old coach from the glory days in Phoenix—it wasn't a smooth, steady rise. Following the loss to the Suns on that February road trip, Bryant had decided to play trainer, questioning whether Howard, suffering with a torn labrum in his shoulder, was really as incapacitated as everyone thought: "Dwight has never been hurt. The [back injury last season] was debilitating and he couldn't play," he told ESPN.com "When you have an injury that hurts you but you can play through it, that's something you have to balance out and manage and he's never really had to do that."

Nash chimed in as well: "I think everyone has got to play through some pain in this league."

Howard, naturally, wasn't happy about it. "He's not a doctor. I'm not a doctor. So that's [Bryant's opinion]," he told reporters. "I mean, I want to play. But at the same time, this is my career, this is my future, this is my life. I can't leave that up to anybody else because nobody else is going to take care of me.

"If people are [ticked] off that I don't play, that I do

play, whatever it may be, so what? This is my career. If I go down, then what? Everybody's life is going to go on."

That this dust-up took place only a few weeks after Howard, with the media present, had stomped around the Lakers' dressing room complaining loudly about his lack of shots as evidenced by the stat sheet, further suggested that things weren't exactly peachy.

But somehow the Lakers stumbled on, running up a respectable 4–2 record on the road trip before a nationally televised showdown at home against the Miami Heat. Despite the tension in the locker room, when the circus hit South Beach it looked like maybe, just maybe, a corner was getting turned. Early in the third quarter the Lakers were leading the defending champions. Could things be looking up?

Maybe not. With the 2012–13 Lakers, every step forward brought at least another step back. For example: There was Nash with the ball under the Heat basket clearly trapped by two defenders and in need of help. And yet, there was Howard in the middle of the key, clearly open, if only Nash could somehow thread the ball through the two defenders—especially challenging given his back was to Howard. A stalemate of sorts ensued—never advisable in a basketball game. Howard didn't move. Nash didn't give him the ball. Eventually, facing a certain turnover, Nash did try and make a pass to Howard, which was promptly deflected, intercepted and in about two seconds converted into a fast-break layup by LeBron James. The game was tied; the Lakers would never lead again.

Adding to the moment, underlining the team's whole failure, was the angry shouting match that broke out between Howard and Nash at half court, captured on national television.

"This is the garbage you can't have," said Jeff Van Gundy on the broadcast. "You can get into it, but it's just happening too often."

Nash later tried to downplay the confrontation during a calm moment in El Segundo: "I'm sure pretty much every point guard in this league has barked at someone this year . . . It's the Napoleon in me. It's totally part of the game. I've barked at a few guys in the past. It's basketball. It's an emotional sport, you're out there fighting. There's a million things going on. Who knows if you had a good night's sleep or your girlfriend's giving you a hard time or what. Guys are emotional and fighting out there and sometimes it gets the better of us. Everyone on our team has gotten pissed at someone at one time or another and that's the way the game is."

Not necessarily. This is the same player a Phoenix Suns intern once counted giving 239 high-fives to his teammates in the course of a single game. During the Heat game, Suns broadcaster Tom Leander, watching from afar, tweeted: "Wow! Never saw Steve ONCE yell @ mate during game. Always positive. That's a mess in L.A."

Were the Lakers the one teamwork riddle that Nash couldn't solve? It was beginning to look that way.

When the news that Nash and Howard were being added to a lineup just two years removed from back-to-back championships and three straight trips to the NBA Finals, optimism ran high, for obvious reasons. Howard, even coming off the back surgery that had brought an early end to his last, tumultuous season in Orlando, was considered the best defensive centre in the NBA. Further, Howard averaged 1.38 points per possession on pick-and-roll plays according the MySynergySports.com data in his last year in Orlando, best in the NBA. And while Nash wasn't playing at quite the level he had during his MVP years, he was still capable of tremendous basketball, having led the NBA in assists for the sixth time in 2011–12. The potential in teaming Nash, perhaps the best pick-and-roll point guard the league had ever seen, with Howard, whose quickness and power had made him one of the best pick-and-roll big men in the game, added to the excitement. If anything, the only point of concern seemed to be how Nash would mesh with Bryant, or, more accurately, how Bryant would mesh with everyone else. As the NBA's acknowledged alpha male, Bryant had already driven away Shaquille O'Neal, upsetting a partnership that had delivered three straight titles from 2000 to 2002. Widely respected as the NBA's fiercest competitor and a tireless professional, Bryant was also seen as someone whose perfectionist bent made being his teammate a trial by fire rather than an exercise in building bonds and maximizing individual strengths.

"Do people like playing with you?" Bryant was asked at one point during the season.

"Probably not, but you'd like the results," he said. "But it depends on your personality. If you're a guy that's demanding of yourself and likes the pressure and the hard work every day, yeah, it's been fun. Everyone is going to get their feelings hurt [at some point] but it's a matter of: Do you have the competitiveness and the drive to meet the expectations that I put on you to be successful and do what we need you to do to be successful? If you can't stand that, if you can't measure up to that, you're going to have a hard time."

Well then.

Paul Shirley is better known as a writer than a basketball player. His book *Can I Keep My Jersey?* chronicles his life on the fringes of the pro game during a career in which he managed eighteen NBA games over three seasons while also bouncing around some of the top leagues in Europe. Having gone to training camp with the Lakers and played a half season with the Suns in Nash's first magical year in Phoenix, he was well positioned to assess the All-Star team being put together in Los Angeles. He wasn't particularly optimistic.

"It's an interesting experiment when you try to put all of these stars together," he said before the season started. "In basketball it's a little different because sometimes you can overwhelm people with raw talent, but if things start to go awry [in L.A.], will that be a failure and will it be because it was an inorganic mixture of players?"

At the time, it was a possibility most people didn't think worth mentioning, but Shirley posited that the Lakers were almost ensured of a clash between two colliding basketball philosophies: Nash's hoops socialism vs. Bryant's rugged individualism. In basketball terms it was a battle of positive and negative.

"My first ever training camp was with the Lakers and it was unpleasant at best," said Shirley. "There's a contrast between [Minnesota and later Boston star] Kevin Garnett and Kobe Bryant. I was in camp with the T-Wolves, too, and Garnett is fairly mean to you at the beginning. He will test you out and find out if you're mentally and physically tough enough to be worthy of his time and respect. But then there's a softening that happens once you're kind of 'in' with him.

"With Kobe there's never that sense of security. He's gotten better at hiding it, but you'll still see where he'll just punk guys out when they screw up, which isn't a recipe for success in basketball, hockey or any sport. It tears people down at the core."

As Nash entered this final phase of his career, the larger question became whether the approach he brought to his first decade and a half in the NBA would hold him in good stead for this last rodeo.

Consider Shirley's assessment of Nash's effect on the Suns when he arrived there in the fall of 2004. The Suns, coming off a 29–53 season, were in need of transformation, but no one predicted Nash would pull it off by himself.

"One of my lingering favourite things about basketball is how much you can tell about a human being based on the way he treats other players," says Shirley, who retired from the game in 2007. "If you look at Nash, he's like the good quarterback. He's the Tom Brady who will throw the ball to you on the next down even when you drop the pass the play before because he understands it's better for him to have you in a good emotional state.

"That season [2004–05], I had just come from Russia, which was mega mercenary—you had guys on the team making 1.2 and 1.5 million euros, which is a lot for a European team. But I turned down 55,000 euros a month because I wanted to leave so badly because I hated everyone on my team. I disliked it so much I was ready to be done with basketball.

"I got home and the Suns signed me to the rest of the year, which was amazing. And when I arrived in Phoenix the contrast was unbelievable. I wasn't there the year before, but they had had a tough year, and [now] I was there to watch this transformation, and you could kind of see it in everyone's eyes: 'Oh . . . we can kind of be nice to each other?'

"It sounds almost hokey, or airy-fairy, but you could see this blooming or opening of everyone's chest and you could see their souls kind of coming to the light. Whereas before—and on most teams—everyone kind of nips at each other and guys are afraid to be nice because it might come back to haunt them."

At his best Nash allowed his teammates to revisit their innocent sides, where basketball wasn't subject to the kind of office politics and workplace Sturm und Drang that make professional sports more like a conventional job than most people realize. With Nash setting the tone, a basketball team could become just that; akin to what most people experience playing sports as kids, or even better: like being part of a supportive, high-achieving family.

"[That innocence] is a very powerful thing," says Shirley. "And the important thing is it's so rare. I [didn't come] across it very often. What's shocking to me is that teams never seem to learn what it means to have a personality like that when it comes to your point guard. Football people get this: if you don't have the right quarterback everything else kind of falls apart. Steve is the ultimate point guard to me because of all of that. Obviously he has the ability, but he's also got this sixth sense for keeping guys together, making them feel a part of the team, whether it's me as the twelfth man at the end of the bench or Amar'e Stoudemire running pick-and-rolls.

"That is a skill he developed early on that is significantly more important than vertical leap but is difficult to measure and we can only see it subjectively, so it's hard to quantify, but it's real," says Shirley.

"When I showed up in training camp with the Suns, I'd played the year before with the Bulls and so maybe a couple of people knew who I was, but generally I was this unknown, big, goofy white guy coming in. And I can vividly remember being in Flagstaff for training camp and getting passes from Steve and not only were they perfect passes that would arrive at the perfect time . . . he would keep throwing even me the ball.

"I had gone to training camp with other teams and the point guards would almost always be like, 'This guy's new and if he misses a shot he's not going to get the ball the rest of training camp.'

"But with Nash, even with me, a guy who's fighting for a spot, he just makes the right play. He doesn't care. He's very democratic—almost socialist—about distributing the ball.

"But also he understands that it breeds a sense of openness among everyone. People are like, 'If he's throwing the ball to Shirley that probably means if I get open he'll certainly throw it to me because my name is Quentin Richardson and I have a little bit better reputation as a shooter than Paul Shirley. What comes off as this altruistic move by throwing it to the last guy on the bench actually has some benefit for everyone.'"

But the Lakers weren't Nash's team, and wouldn't ever be. Bryant was more than the Lakers' best player, he was the boy prince who had matured into the franchise king. Acquired on draft night in 1997 by the great Jerry West, Bryant had waged wars and won titles using his endless arsenal of one-on-one moves to remain one of basketball's elite scorers even as age ever-so-slowly chipped away at his dominant athleticism. Among the alarm bells that went off early in Mike Brown's brief tenure was that rather than use Nash to initiate offence with the ball, creating advantages in the pick-and-roll—the aspect of the game at which Nash was a master and the reason he is surely headed to the Hall of Fame—Brown opted to make him one player among five in an equal-opportunity, read-and-react offence. More often than not Nash would advance the ball, deliver a first pass, cut through the lane to the far side of the floor and not see the ball again. Things were further complicated when in the second game of the season, Nash had collided with Damian Lillard, the dynamic rookie point guard with the Portland Trail Blazers. When D'Antoni came aboard a few games later, Nash was sidelined with a hairline fracture of his fibula and a bruised nerve. He was out of the lineup for twenty-four games in total, including the first two months of D'Antoni's run on the sidelines. By the time he was back in uniform, there wasn't much hope of the Lakers becoming anything other than what they had always been: Kobe's team.

On December 22, the night of Nash's return to the lineup, the Lakers were playing the upstart Golden State Warriors, a team led by Steph Curry, a sweet-shooting guard who credited Nash as one of his foremost influences. The Lakers won in dramatic fashion, coming back from 14 points down to win in overtime. And Bryant? As if to mark his territory he took 41 shots, double his season average (which led the league) and 10 more than any other game that season. Bryant scored 34 points and was effusive in his praise of Nash. Playing in his first game in two months, Nash had logged nearly forty minutes, a season high.

"It's easy. It's very easy. It's beyond easy," Bryant said after the game about playing with Nash. "You put two guys together who can do opposite things and it fits extremely well. When I get a rebound, I look to get the ball in his hands because I know I will be getting an easy shot."

Lost in the small type was Dwight Howard's nearly non-existent contribution—8 shots and 11 points in twenty-nine minutes. It went unsaid that as long as the moon revolved around Bryant, everything was just fine. But as time wore on it was proving an awkward way to play basketball, and not quite the way Nash believes the game should be played. In the Lakers one visit to Toronto, Nash was less than cryptic in his assessment of how the team was coming together.

"Obviously Kobe is used to playing one-on-one, but I've got to say, it's been a pleasure to play with Kobe," he said. "I know he's extremely competitive, he prepares, he fights, and I think there's room for both styles at times. And I think he can really benefit, and we can take a lot of pressure off him if we just run the system, and he doesn't have to come down and go against the other team all the time.

"But if we don't get to our spots and take care of the details offensively, he's going to be stuck getting the ball with a guy on him and the whole team loaded up and every-one standing and watching him. And it's not going to yield high percentages for our team when he has to take on everybody."

Bryant had shot just 10-of-32 from the floor in the Lakers' loss to the lowly Raptors. After, he could only blame himself. "Just point the finger at me," he said. "This one is on me." He then took to his newly opened Twitter account to post a picture of a brick wall and the caption: "Brick City." It prompted Cathal Kelly of the *Toronto Star* to sum up the Lakers' season with the following: "This guy even hogs the *criticism*."

When the need to better integrate Howard into the offence could no longer be ignored, Bryant went so far as to hog assists. In one game against the Los Angeles Clippers he didn't take a shot until midway through the first quarter, instead trying his hand at point guard while Nash stood around and the rest of the Lakers looked like they'd just seen Dad in Mum's underwear. At various points Nash, the master of the pick-and-roll, resorted to setting ball screens for Bryant, his shooting guard, so that Bryant, the protypical finisher, could be the one creating off the dribble. It was Tiger Woods becoming a caddy. The basketball world was upside down.

To Nash's credit, he adjusted. If Bryant wants to handle the ball, he'll set screens and work on his catch-and-shoot game. You can't spend your entire career trying to give your teams exactly what they need and then throw a pout when a particular group of teammates doesn't want to do things exactly the way you do them best, even if it might be best for all concerned. It turns out Howard was uncomfortable running pick-and-rolls with Nash, preferring to get his offence off post-ups on the block. With the writing on the wall and a playoff spot in doubt, Nash kept his head down and chipped away at the task. In some ways it was as impressive a team-first gesture as anything he'd ever done. In a lineup full of All-Stars, someone had to take less. When no one volunteered, Nash did.

"I came to the realization that I have to embrace whatever the role is and whatever the team needs and get on with it and be happy and be a good teammate and try to improve in those areas or else we're kidding ourselves. I don't want to be another distraction—and I'm not blaming anybody—we're all trying to figure something out and I don't want to deter us from doing so. I want to help us get there."

It meant watching his numbers slip and having his game questioned by the likes of influential *Los Angeles Times* columnist Bill Plaschke, who wrote of Nash: "He is awful. He is great. He is sometimes slow. He is occasionally sneaky. He is, on the whole, precisely the opposite of the sort of point guard that everyone thought he would be. Steve Nash is ordinary. He is Ramon Sessions. He is Derek Fisher. He is decidedly not Steve Nash. . . .

"From the moment Nash showed up on opening night in a pink sweater and bow tie while carrying a man purse, Los Angeles has seemingly been blinded by his style and his smarts, his pre-game effort, his post-game perspective.

"It's a different story when one actually examines his basketball."

It was a situation Nash hadn't faced since his first year in Dallas, when—having signed a lucrative long-term deal—he hobbled around, hampered by back and hamstring problems that sent him stumbling to the worst season of his professional career. At the time there were boos and doubts, and what could Nash really respond with? It's not like he had a resume of enduring success to draw on and silence his critics. Instead he figured out how to get healthy, sharpen his game and shut his critics up game by game, win by win.

The irony was that now it was just such a resume that was haunting him and he was running out of games to win. He had his standards, but to hear him explain it, Nash wasn't going to let the final years of his career be defined by how they measured up to what came before.

"Am I concerned that I need to live up to something? No. I still have a lot of confidence," he said. "I still feel like I can do pretty much everything I've ever done. I still feel like I show it on a night-to-night basis, just in a very small window. I just don't get a lot of opportunities to do it. But at the same time, for me to sit here and complain about opportunities would further hinder our growth and finding our identity."

Did someone need to be the grown-up?

"I don't want to say that, but just try to keep playing. For me it's important for my well-being to just shut up and play. I just [feel like] come on, do your job and enjoy it and be a source of energy for your team instead of bemoaning the fact that it's not the same as it used to be."

The challenge for Nash was how to be influential when he wasn't the central figure like he had been in Phoenix, or at least a key ally in the cause, the arrangement he shared with Dirk Nowitzki in Dallas. Was there a way for him to find joy in a game he used to control with his quickness, his eyes and his mind; using his individual brilliance to elevate a team? The end comes for every player. As great as the great ones are, they never end on their terms—they end up slower, weaker, less effective. There is no choice in that.

The choice is to remain honourable, throwing everything you have into finding ways to make your exit from the sport as graceful as possible. Nash's first year in Los Angles was a living lesson in maintaining your pride by not being stubbornly prideful. When he first returned from his injury, he played a big part in the Lakers offence as the team's primary ball-handler and averaged 9.2 assists a game. But the Lakers struggled, going just 5-11 in his first 16 games back. At that point a decision was made to slow the Lakers pace down, put the ball in Bryant's hands more and have Nash play more of a shooting guard roll, even if he was a hall-of-fame point guard, a move Nash didn't fight.

"To be a good NBA player you have to have an ego, but the very thing that makes you and makes it all possible can also be a hindrance at times," he says. "A lot of times our greatest strengths are our greatest weaknesses and so, you can't have it all. You have to go through some growing pains. You have to go through times when you have to figure things out. You can't not have an ego in this league or it will be a short run, and you can't ask people to be egoless at other times. That's not what it's all about. It's just sometimes so ingrained in you to do what you've done your whole life to change."

By most measures, Nash's first season in Los Angeles was a failure. The Lakers struggled all year long and Nash played just 50 of 82 games, the most games he lost to injury in a season in his entire career. They were swept in the playoffs and Nash was a non-factor as the hip and hamstring problems that he has always trained so carefully to keep at bay began tormenting him. He missed the last eight games of the regular season even as the Lakers playoff hopes hinged in the balance. He finally had a series of cortisone and epidural shots in order to be able to play in the playoffs against the San Antonio Spurs, but had to shut himself down after two games playing at decidedly less than full speed.

There was some irony in that a player who started his career being overlooked was unable to deliver when he was finally such a sought-after commodity. But Nash remained undeterred. There were those who wondered if his troubling season was his body's last gasp and if retirement was the proper path. Nash, once again was unwanted in some corners, as Lakers fans and media lamented the drag the remaining two years and $18 million would have on the team's already bloated salary structure. In some ways it was perfect however. Being unwanted had always brought out his best and now he had the motivation that had always lifted him front and centre again. There were calls for him to quit. For Nash it was a signal to get going. "I'm definitely going to prepare better than I ever had to try to make this year a distant memory," he said as the Lakers packed up their lockers. "And [make] next year a phenomenal experience."

Typical. Nash has never shied away from the road less travelled, even when it's uphill. He embarked on a journey to become an NBA player with nearly every conceivable reason to fail immediately in front of his face. He wasn't very big and not incredibly fast and he wasn't from a place that NBA players are supposed to come from and he barely got a scholarship at a school that had almost no track record of producing elite professional talent. Then he didn't become an All-Star until he was 28 years old and he didn't win a Most Valuable Player award until he was 30. By the time Nash signed his last NBA contract, the list of players that had reached stardom and disappeared within the span of his career included the likes of Allen Iverson, Stephon Marbury and Tracy McGrady. Countless others who'd entered the league to much greater fanfare never made the kind of impact their talent suggested: Steve Francis, Darko Milicic, Jay Williams, T. J. Ford—the list goes on.

You want full circle? How about this: the end of Nash's career will not be all that different from the start and many stages along the way; the shadow of doubt ever present. The difference between the beginning and the ending— regardless of how or when it ends—is that Nash will always have the years in between as a testament to the power that comes from pushing yourself for the benefit of those who wear the same jersey, who need you to think of the team first and get them the ball.

The testimonials are everywhere, secured forever in MVP trophies and All-Star berths; in 60-win seasons and a basketball aesthetic that captured the imagination of fans and helped change the game. But perhaps it's best expressed by a teammate, one of the 124 (and counting) Nash delivered the ball to in just the right way, at just the right time on his way to 10,000 career assists.

Marcin Gortat was a soccer goalie from Poland before taking up basketball, which wasn't a bad choice given he was 6-foot-11 and could run and jump and bang big bodies with enthusiasm. But in four seasons with the Orlando Magic, he couldn't score, or not very well, as he averaged just 5.7 points a game. He was traded to Phoenix in the summer before the 2009–10 season—into the orbit of Steve Nash. His life changed. The ball materialized. He scored and he was appreciated. He had fun, and when his next contract comes up he will likely get paid very well, given he averaged a very respectable 14.4 points a game in two seasons with Nash.

If Nash ever needs help moving on a hot summer weekend, he should call Gortat. He would likely be among the first in a long line of ex-teammates who would show up. "One day I'm going to write a book, and a huge chapter in that book is going to be about playing with Steve . . . being honest with you, right now this guy is a legend," says Gortat, his Polish accent lightly inflected with hip-hop cadences. "Some players can tell their kids, 'I had an opportunity to play with Michael Jordan, I had an opportunity to play with this big player or that big player.' I'm going to say I had an opportunity to play with Steve Nash. That's how I feel about him. Tremendous professional player, always ready to play, always focused. Everything he does he does with heart, with passion.

"He's a true leader, he never puts anyone down. When someone is down he's already trying to pick them up and build them up. When he has to yell at someone he will, but if he doesn't have to he picks them up. Being honest with you? True freaking role model. That's how I see him."

It's a view widely shared, and with good reason.

ACKNOWLEDGEMENTS

The authors would like to thank Craig Pyette at Random House Canada, an expert editor whose patience and guidance are always appreciated.

Credit is also due to our many colleagues in the sportswriting business whose work has informed our thinking and buttressed this book with helpful insights and archival quotations. That roster includes Jeff Rud, who told Nash's story in two earlier books, Marc Stein, Paul Coro, Jack McCallum, Chris Ballard, Doug Smith, Dwain Price, Chris Young, Howard Beck, Bruce Arthur, Eric Koreen, Ryan Wolstat, Dave McMenamin, Ed Graney, Henry Abbott, John Hollinger, Chris Sheridan, Jerry Crowe, Cathal Kelly, Dane Huffman, Sean Deveney, Gordon Monson, Bob Young, Bob Baum, Brian Hutchinson and Dan Bickley. And that's just naming a few.

Thanks to Steve Maich of *Sportsnet* magazine, along with the editors at *The Globe and Mail, National Post* and *Toronto Star* for their support in our reporting on Nash throughout his career. We owe a debt, too, to Evan Rosser for his careful eye, and to Holly MacKenzie for her keen feedback.

There's a long list of people who gave of their time and knowledge in the phone conversations, courtside chats and locker-room interviews that added so much to our understanding of the main character. Many of those folks are named in these pages, some are not. We send appreciation to all.

Speaking of eternal gratitude—we owe our families at least that, and probably more, for their love and support.

We also owe a nod to Bill Duffy at BDA Sports and Jenny Miller at the Steve Nash Foundation for their assistance over the years. And thanks, especially, to Steve Nash, always a helpful and thoughtful interview subject and always an inspiration.

PHOTO CREDITS

"Stephen Nash . . ." courtesy St. Michaels University School

"As a teenager in Victoria . . ." courtesy St. Michaels University School

"Eli Pasquale . . ." courtesy University of Victoria Archives

"Coach Ken Shields . . ." courtesy University of Victoria Archives

"Directing traffic . . ." courtesy Santa Clara Athletic Department

"In 1996, Nash joins . . ." NBAE/Getty Images

"After a difficult first season . . ." NBAE/Getty Images

"Nash flashes his national . . ." Toronto Star via Getty Images

"In January 2002 . . ." NBAE/Getty Images

"'To compare Steve Nash . . .'" AFP/Getty Images

"He can jump . . ." Sports Illustrated/Getty Images

"Back in Phoenix . . ." NBAE/Getty Images

"Nash and Stoudamire . . ." Sports Illustrated/Getty Images

"Nash goes to the basket . . ." NBAE/Getty Images

"Nash is awarded . . ." Getty Images

"Nowitzki tries in vain . . ." Sporting News via Getty Images

"Only in the NBA . . ." NBAE/Getty Images

"Looking more like . . ." (top) NBAE/Getty Images; (bottom) Getty Images

"These guys love to play . . ." Getty Images

"Nash always had . . ." courtesy University of Victoria Athletic Department

"Can this possibly work . . ." NBAE/Getty Images

INDEX

MICHAEL GRANGE and **DAVE FESCHUK** are the bestselling co-authors of *Leafs AbomiNation: The Dismayed Fan's Guide to Why the Leafs Stink and How They Can Rise Again*. Together they bring some 3 decades of sportswriting experience to this, their second joint effort. Grange, a multi-platform journalist for Rogers Sportsnet since 2011, appears regularly on *Prime Time Sports*, the most-listened-to sports talk show in Canada. Formerly of *The Globe and Mail*, where he covered the NBA and other sports for more than 15 years, he is a senior writer at *Sportsnet Magazine* and an on-air correspondent on Sportsnet's various television outlets. Feschuk, a *Toronto Star* sports columnist since 2003, has been a regular fixture on the pro basketball beat since he joined the *National Post* in 1998. He can be seen and heard frequently on TSN's *Off the Record* and TSN radio.